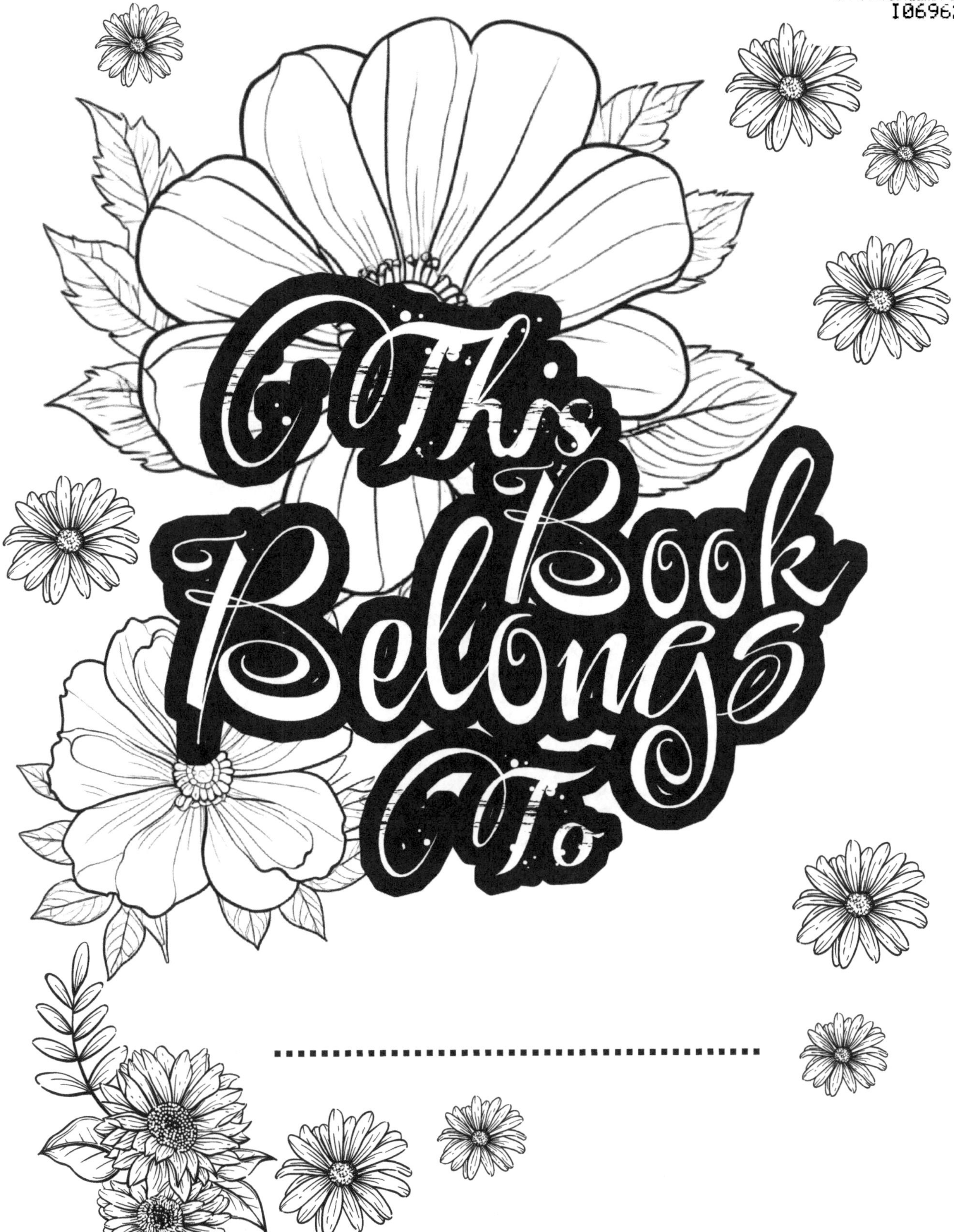

This Book Belongs To

....

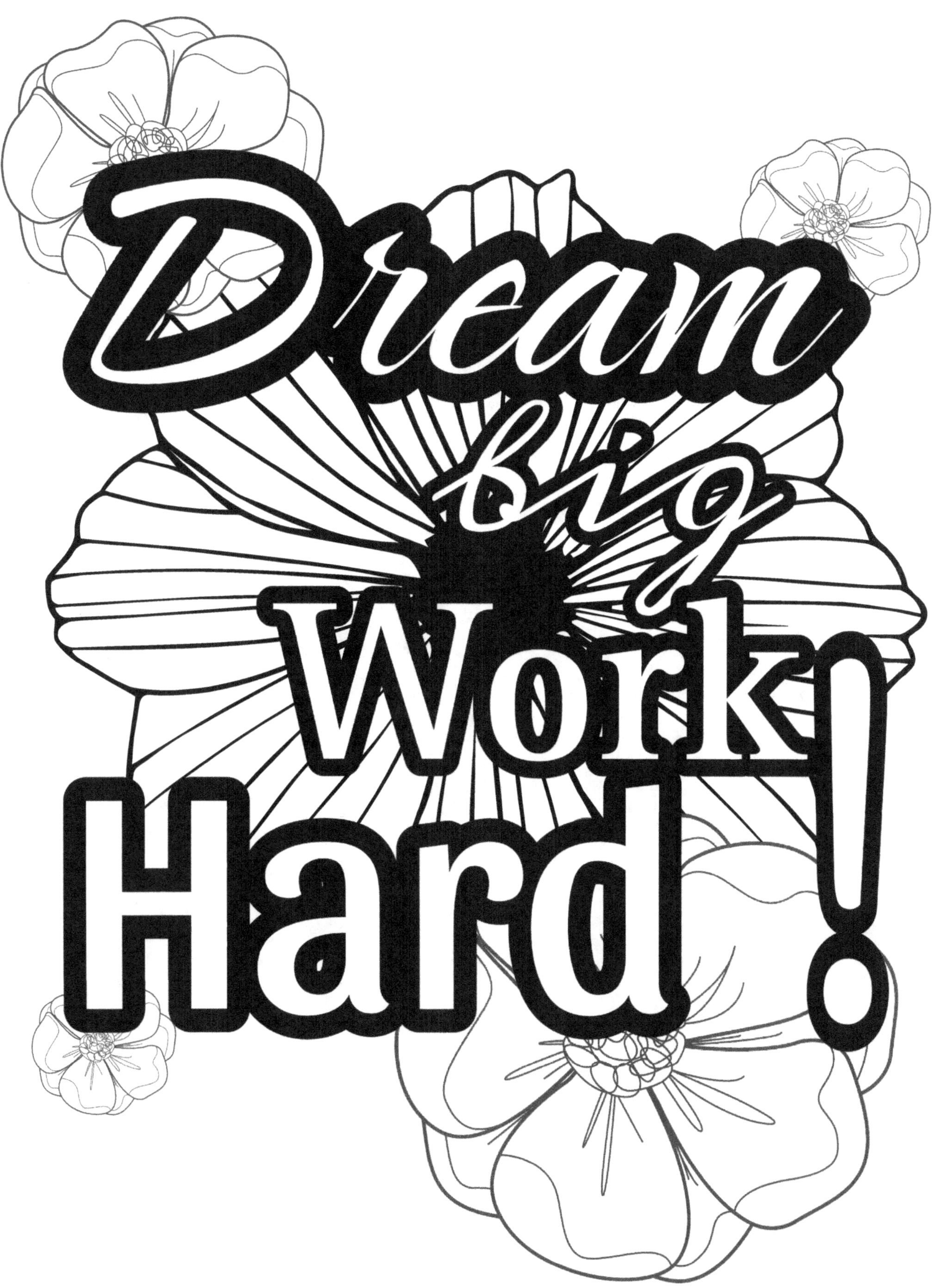

Dream
big
Work
Hard!

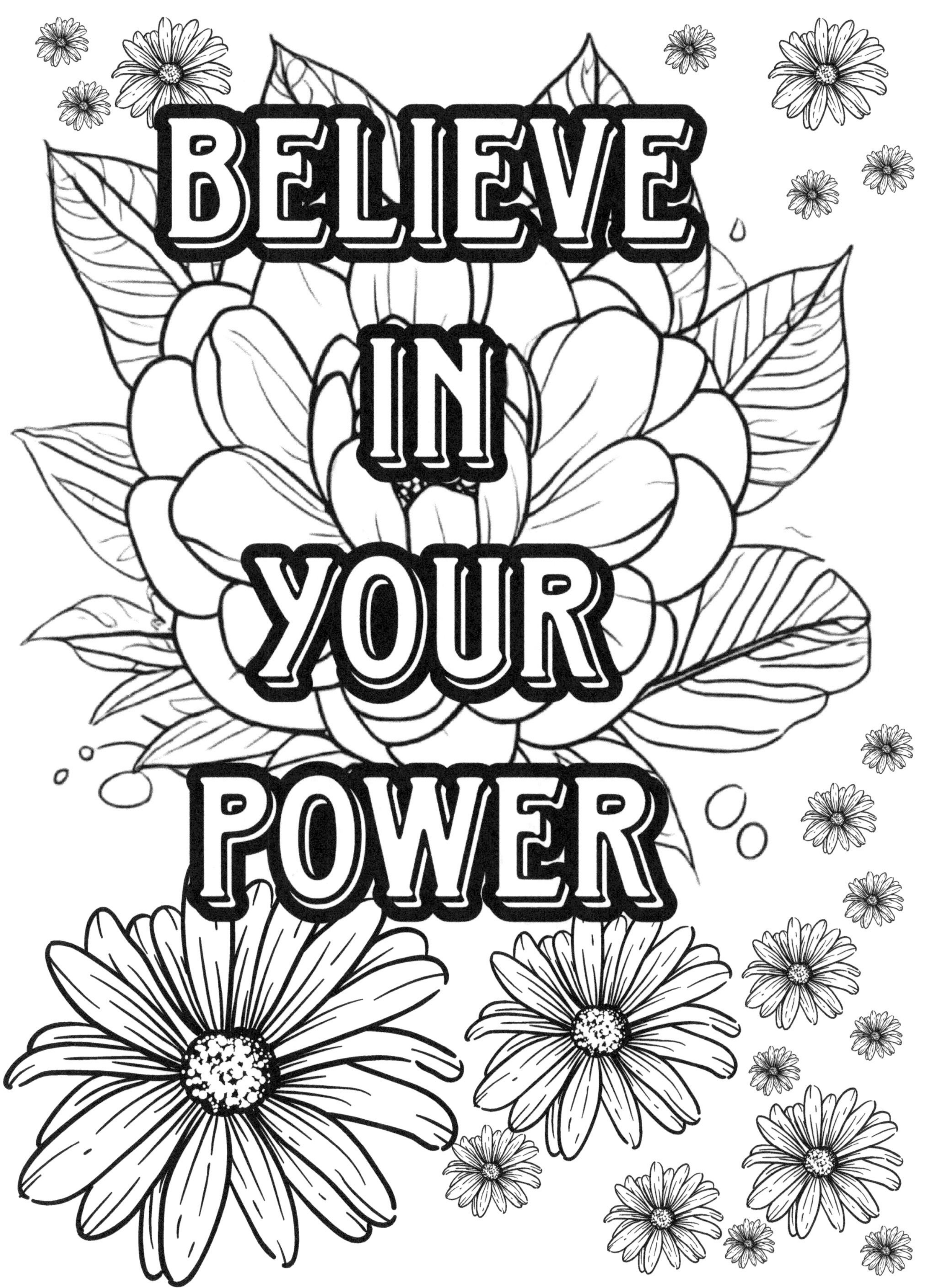

BELIEVE
IN
YOUR
POWER

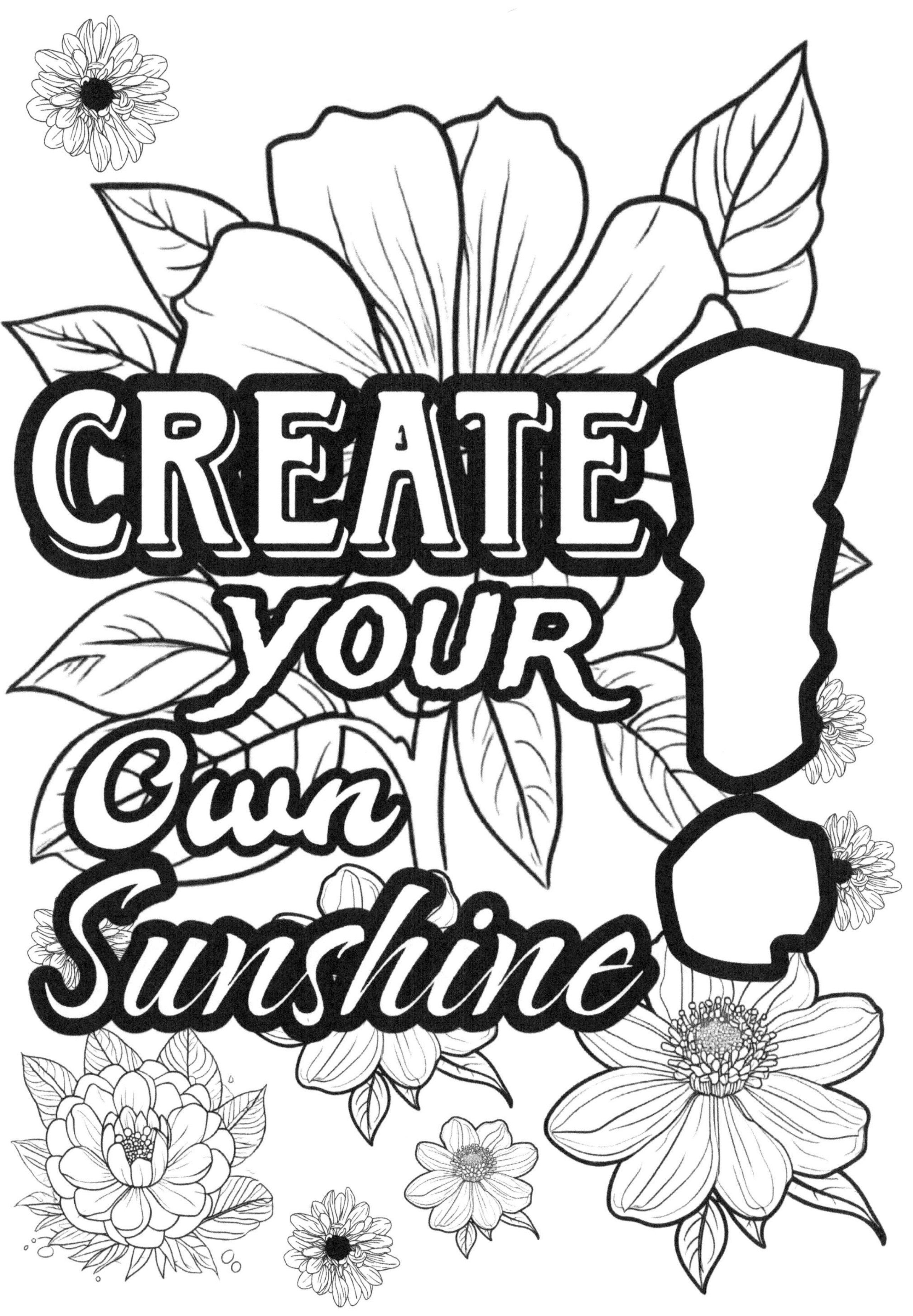

CREATE
YOUR
Own
Sunshine

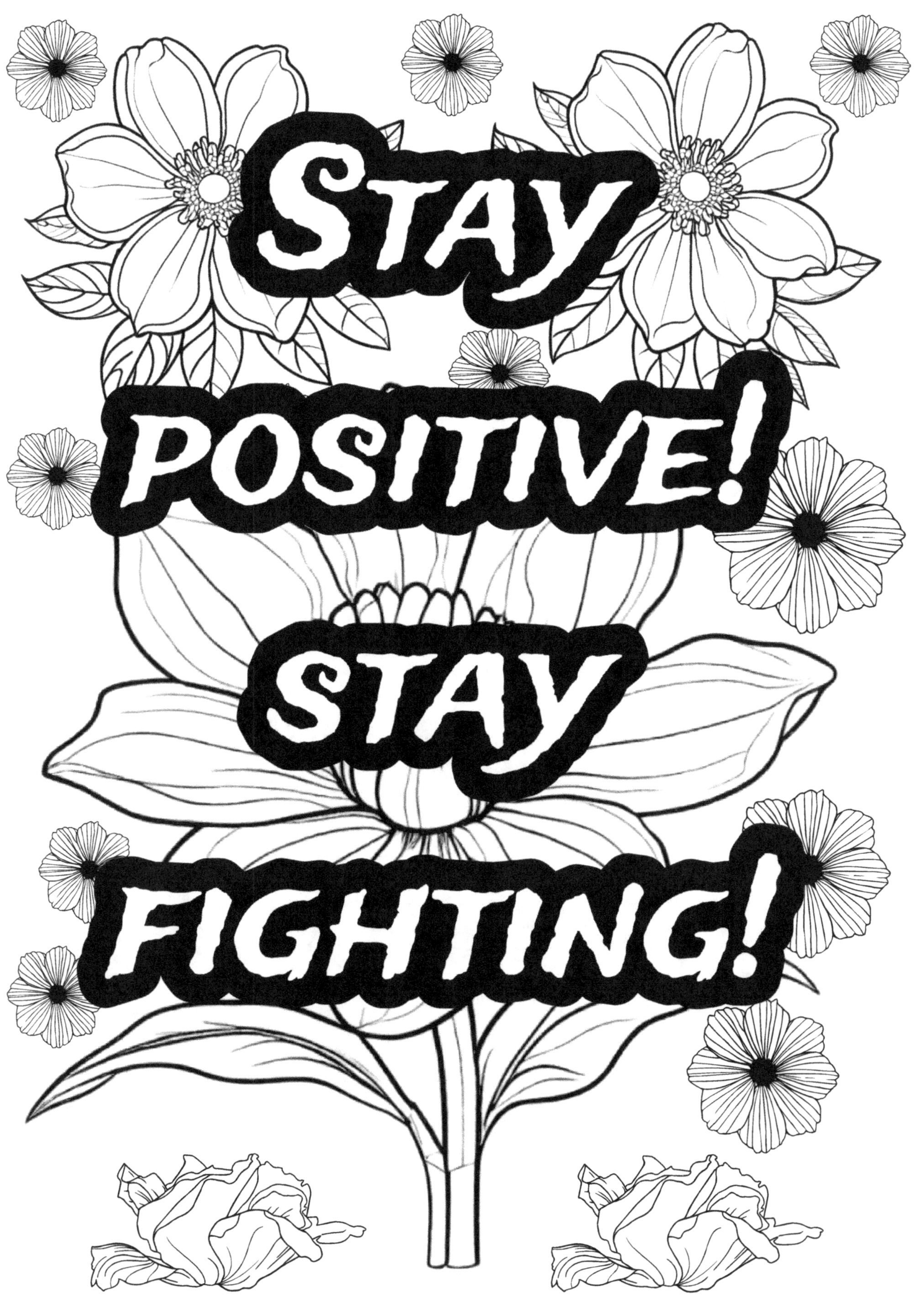

STAY
POSITIVE!
STAY
FIGHTING!

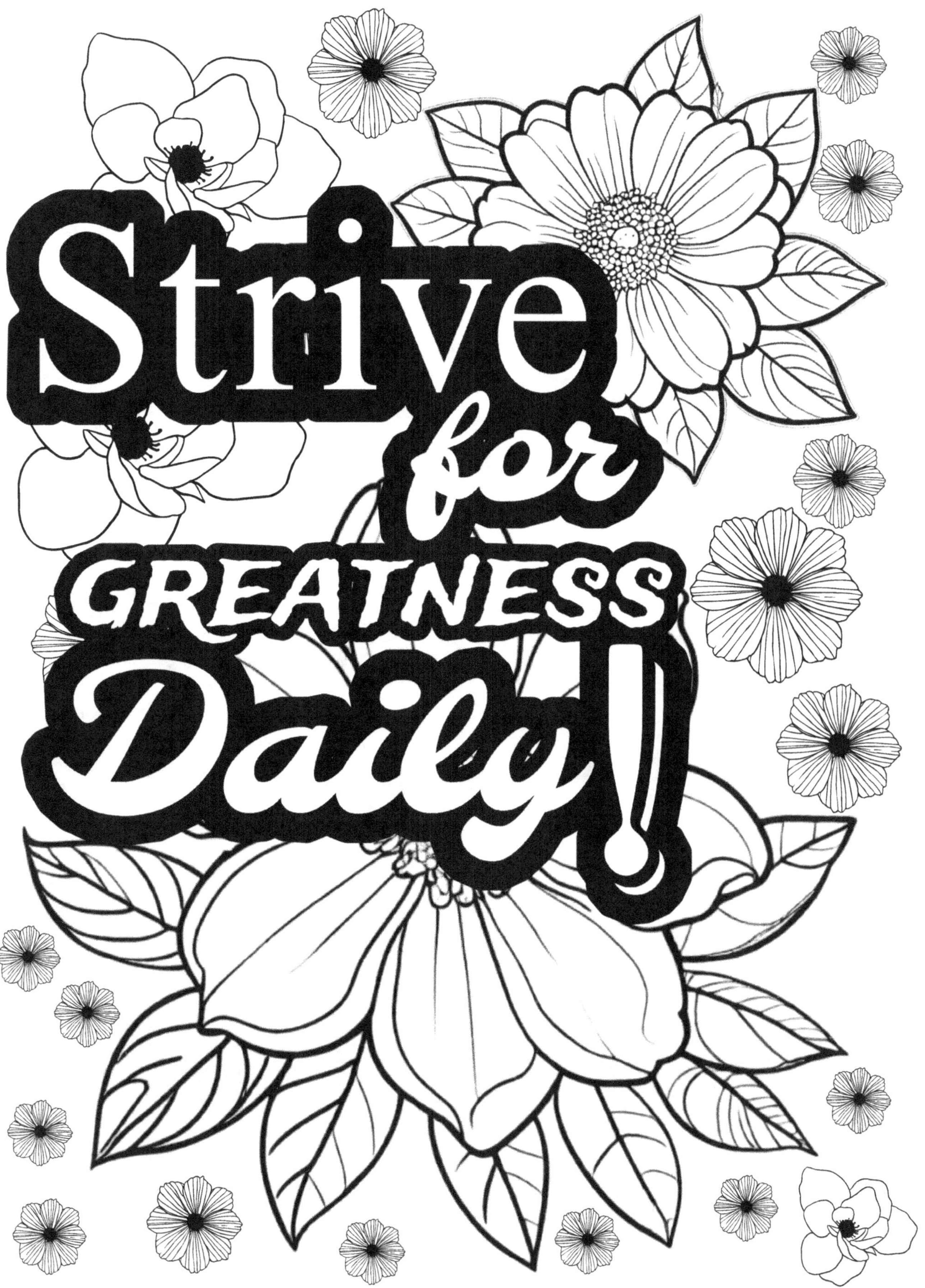
Strive
for
GREATNESS
Daily!

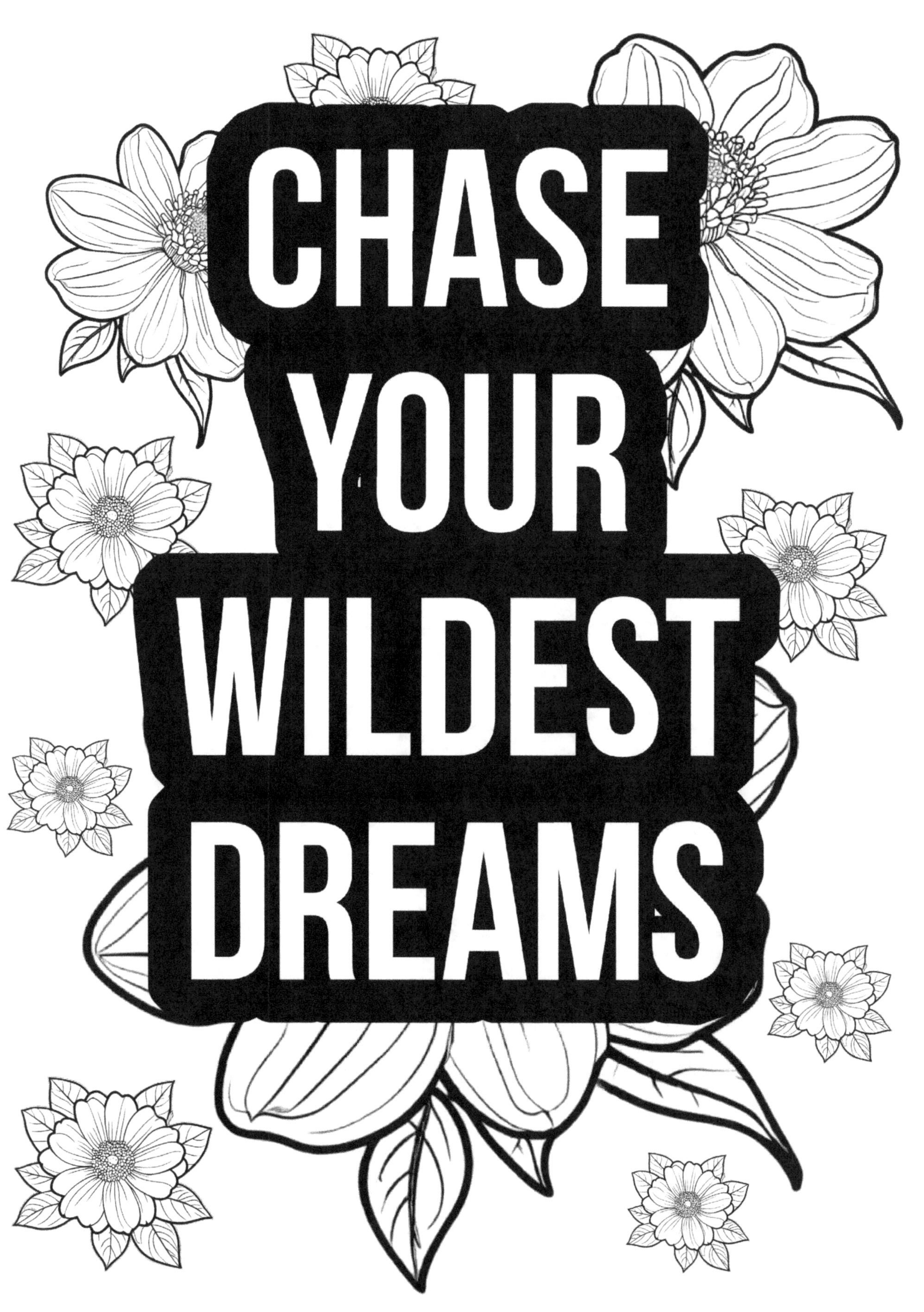

CHASE
YOUR
WILDEST
DREAMS

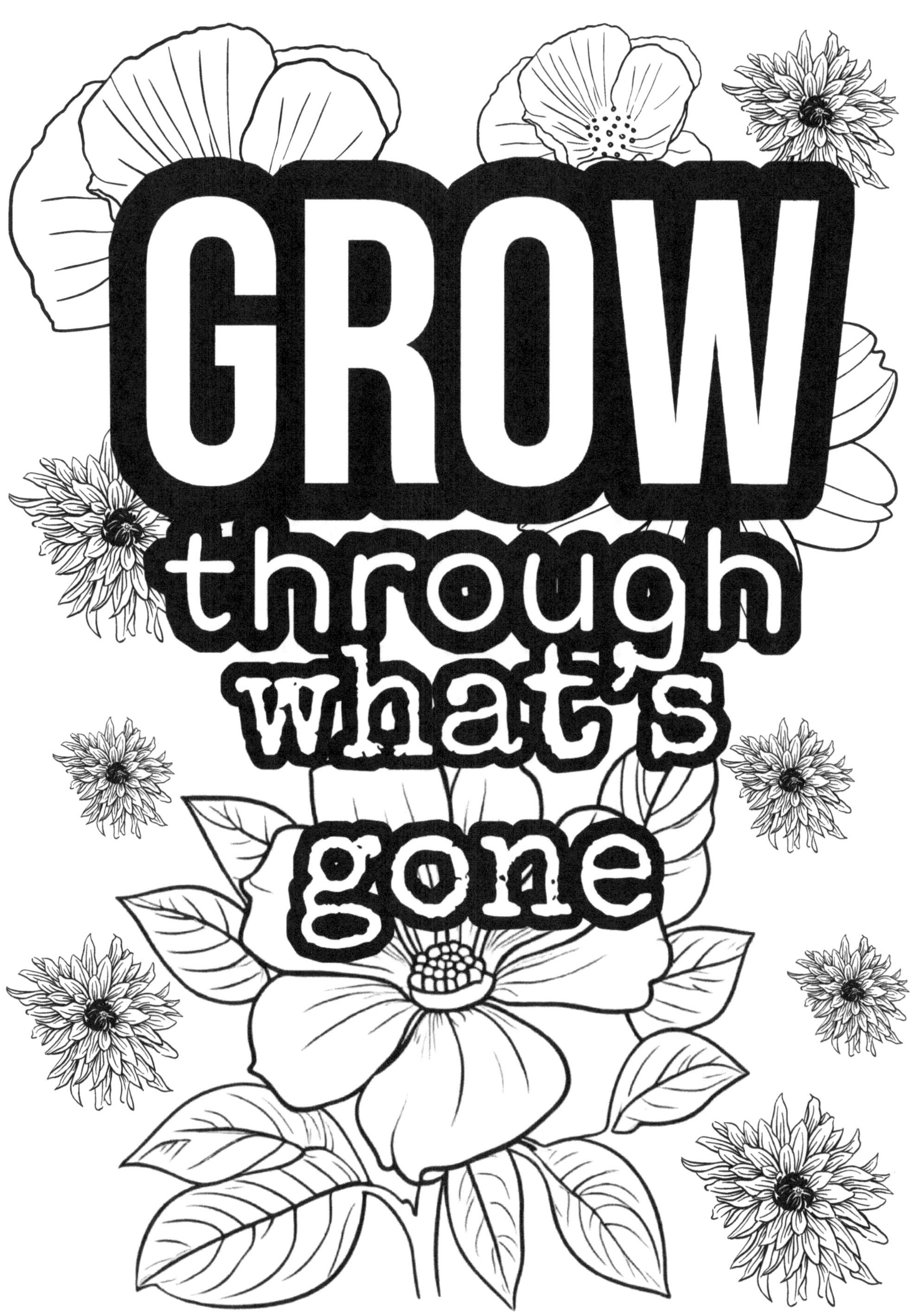

GROW
through
what's
gone

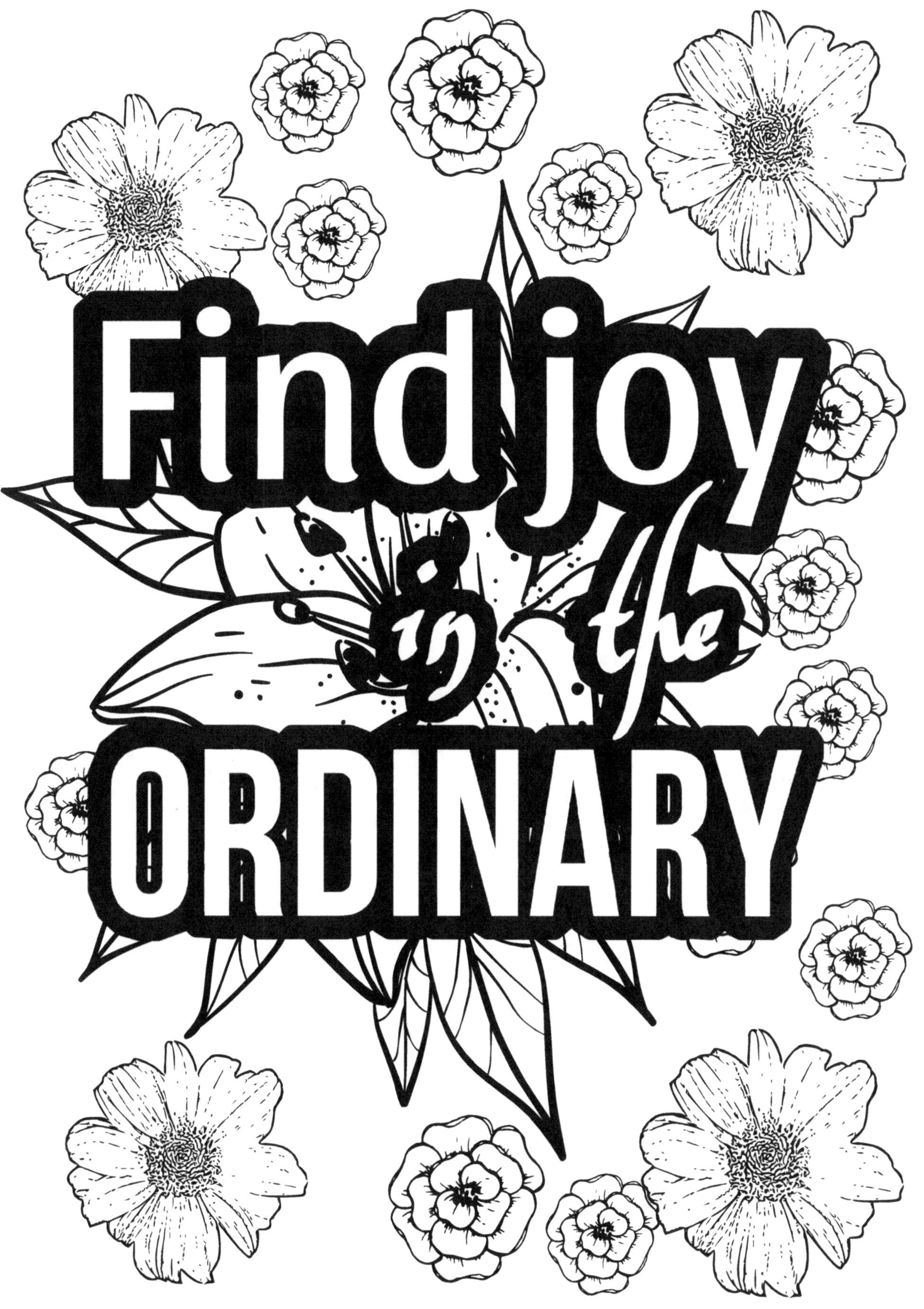

Find joy in the ORDINARY

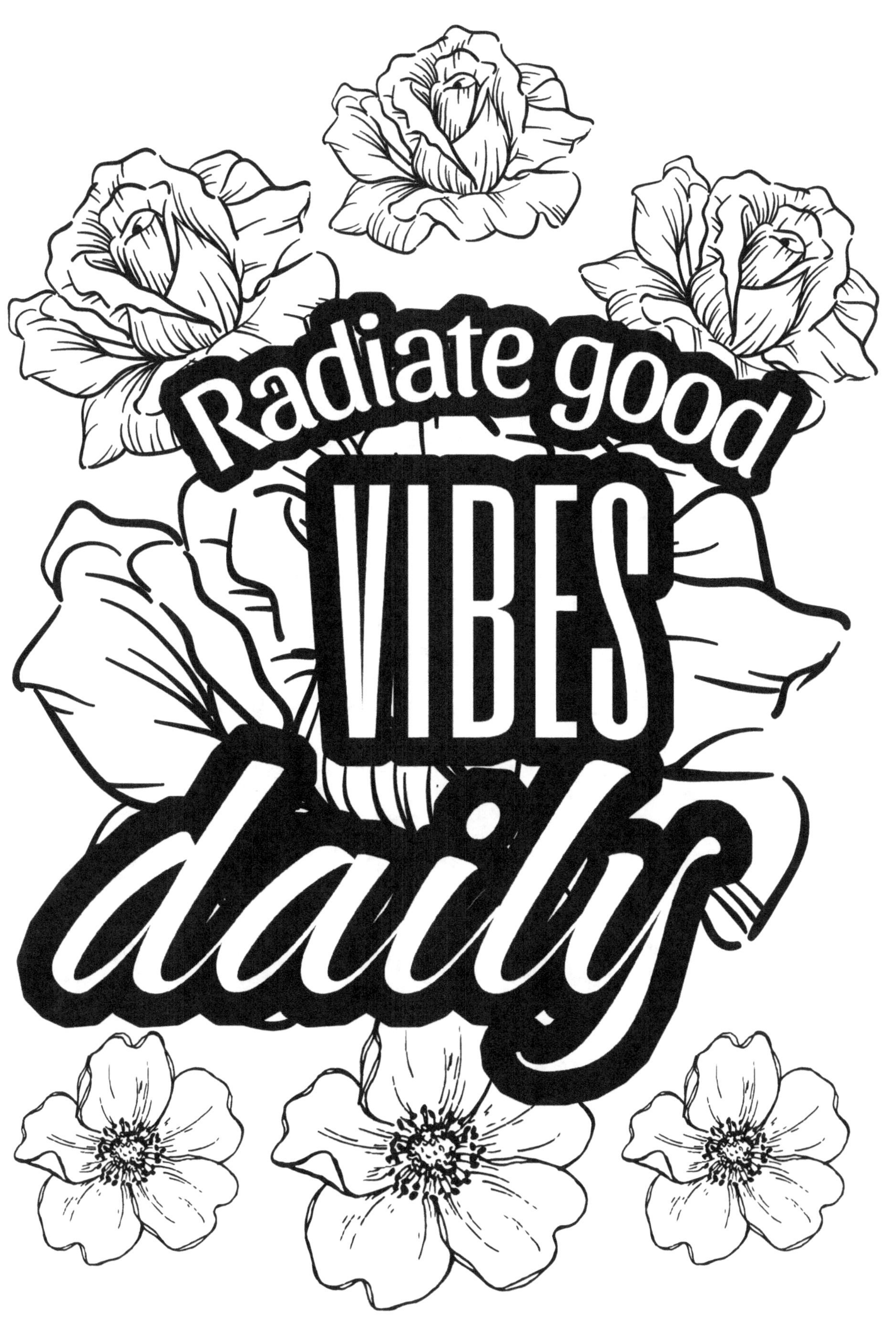

Radiate good
VIBES
daily

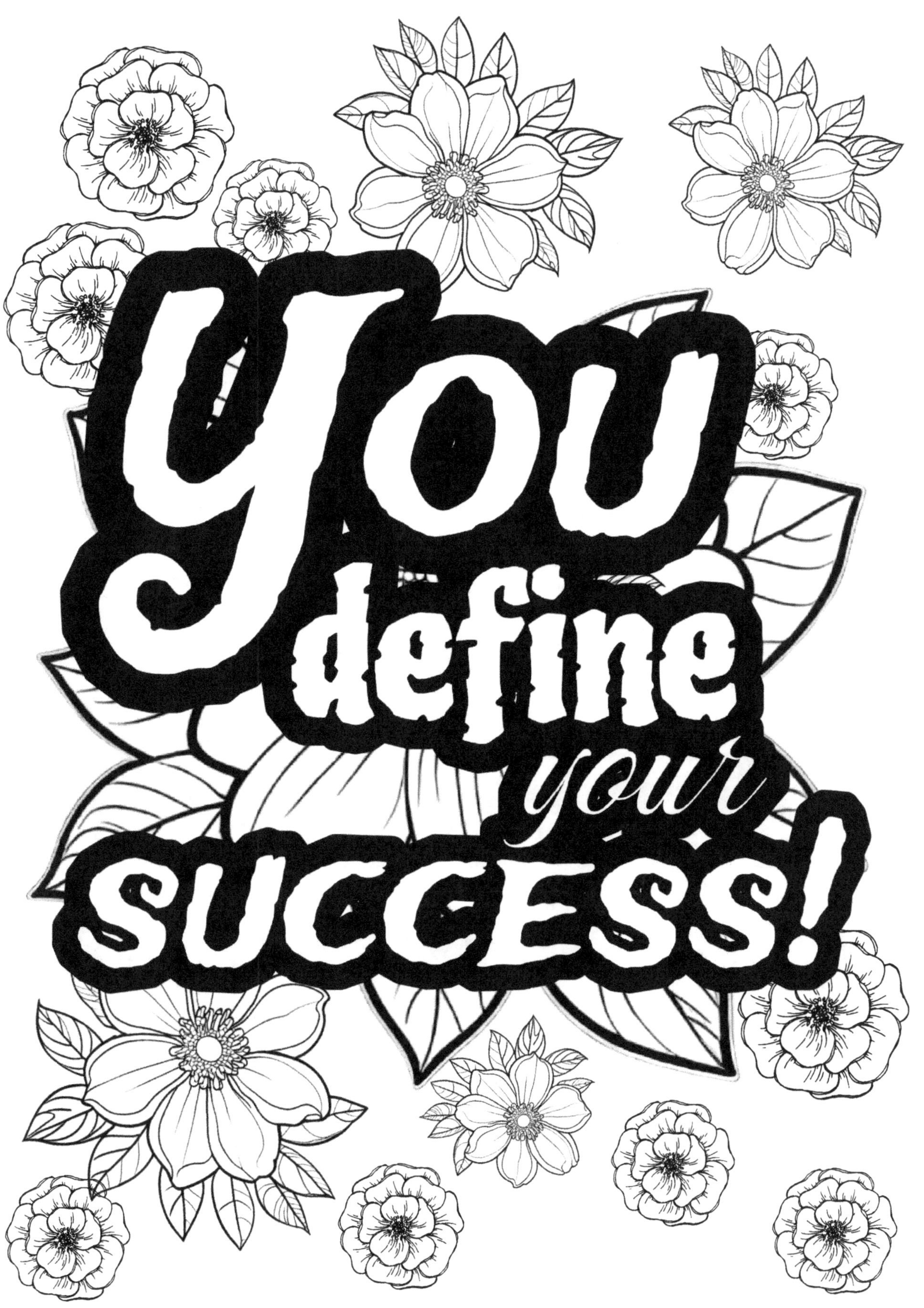

You define your SUCCESS!

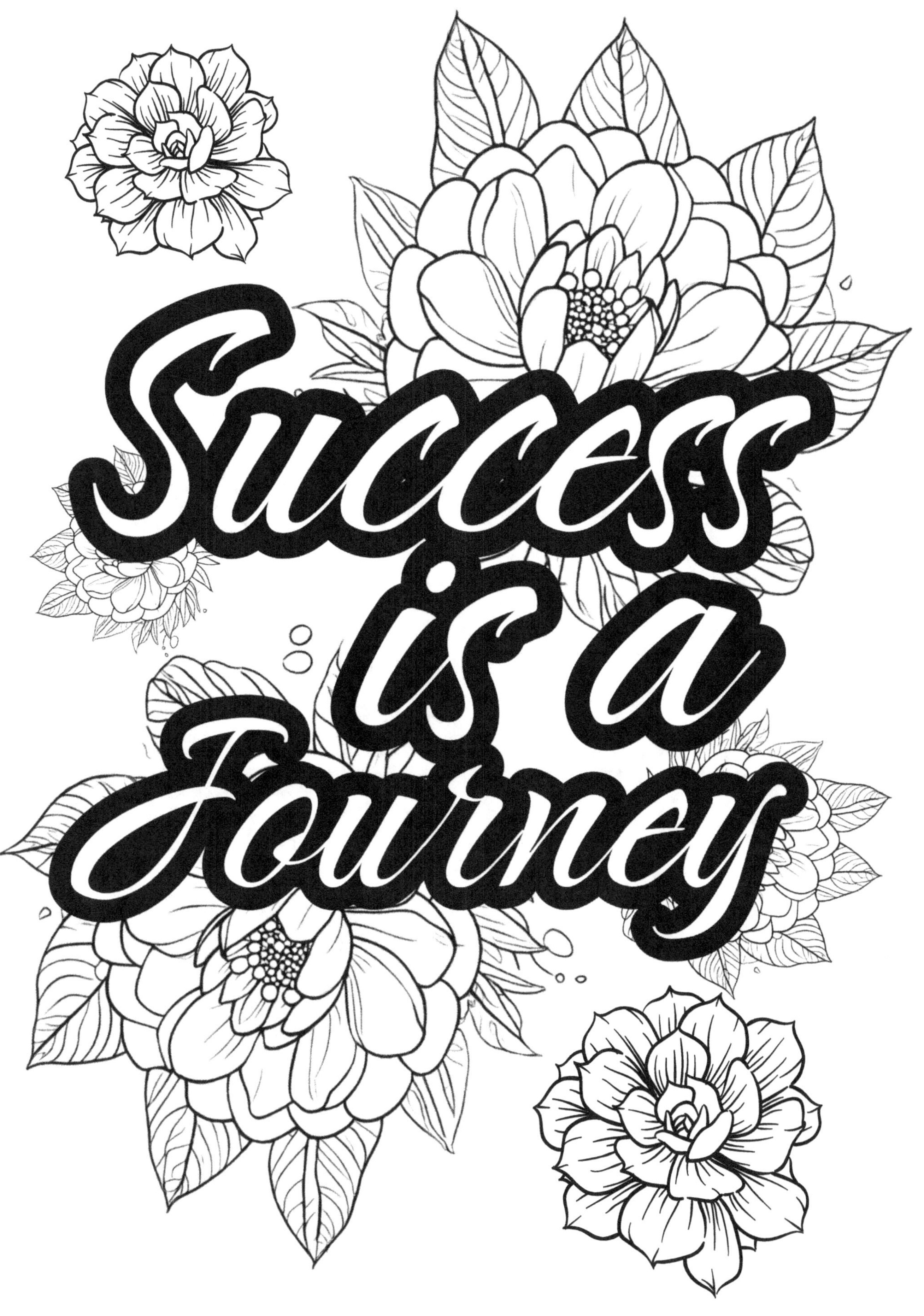
Success
is a
Journey

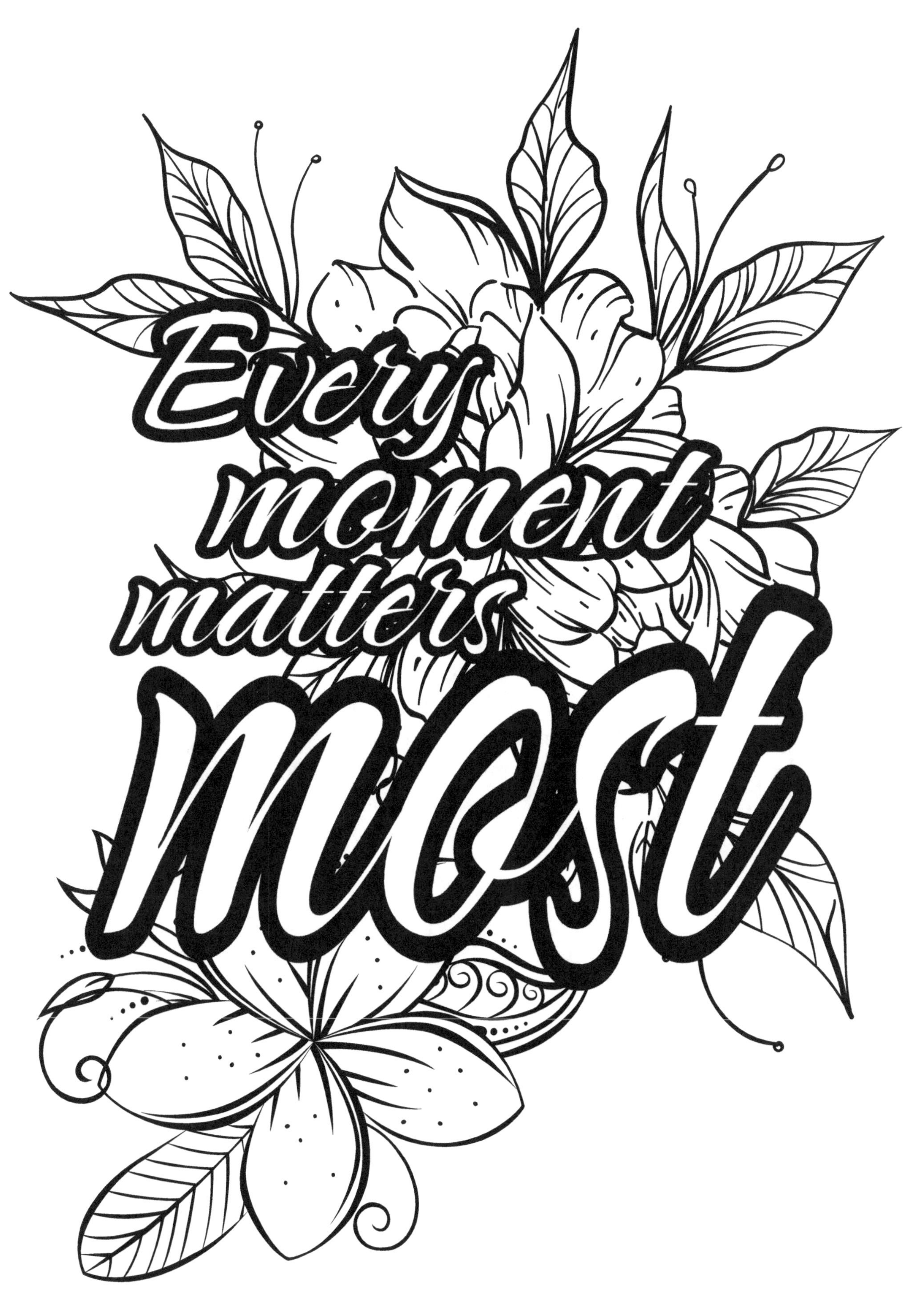

Every
moment
matters
most

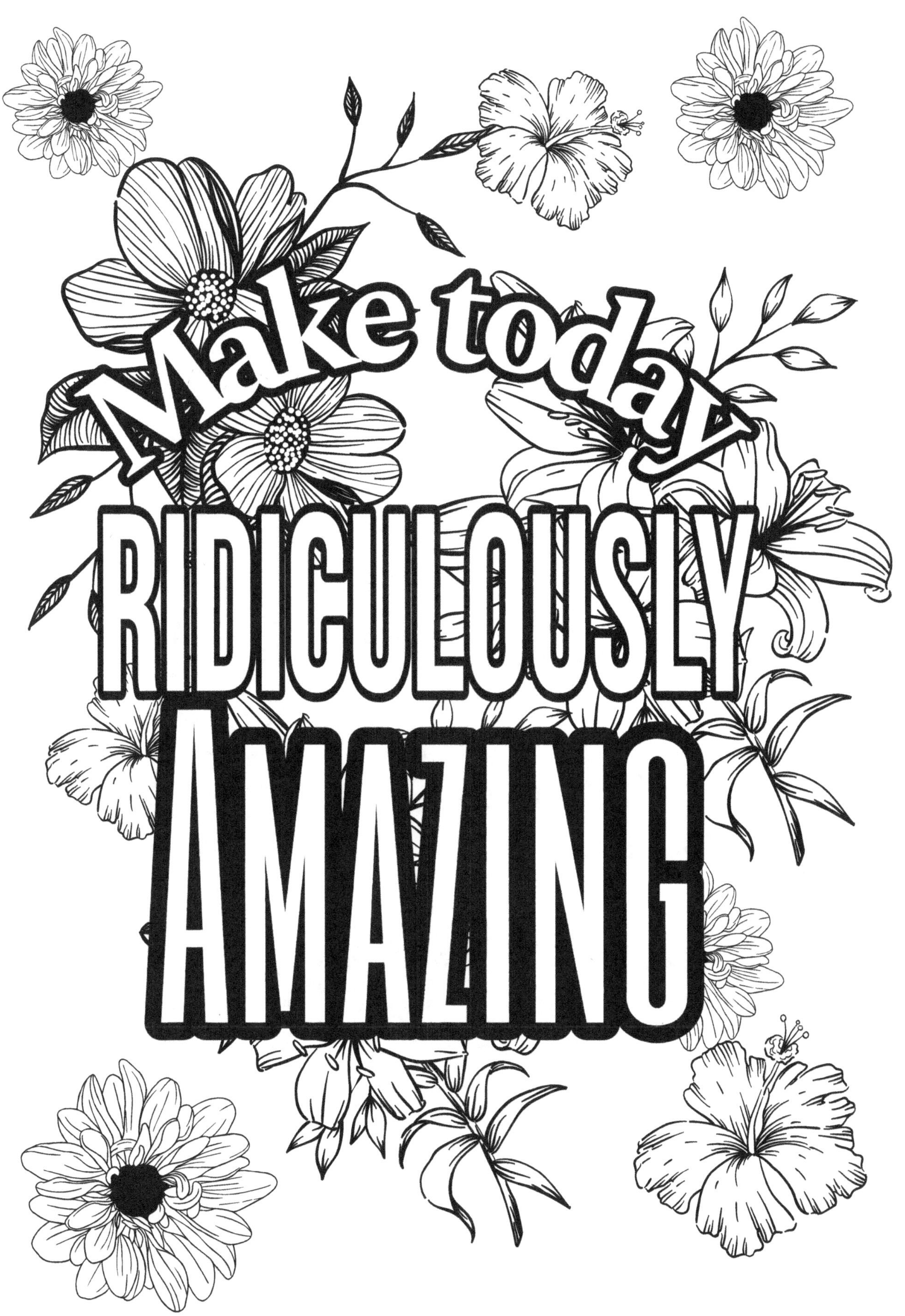

Make today
RIDICULOUSLY
AMAZING

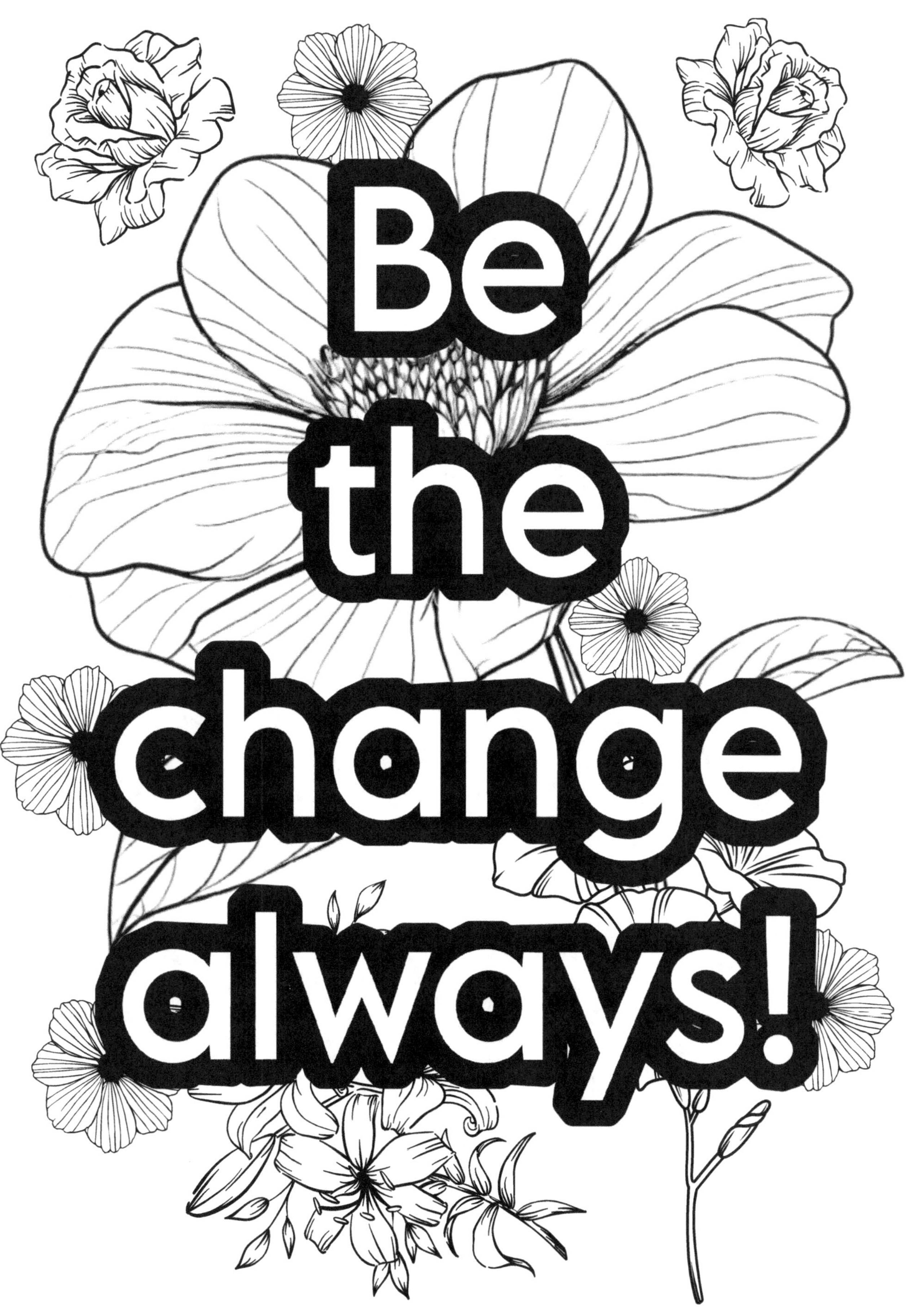
Be
the
change
always!

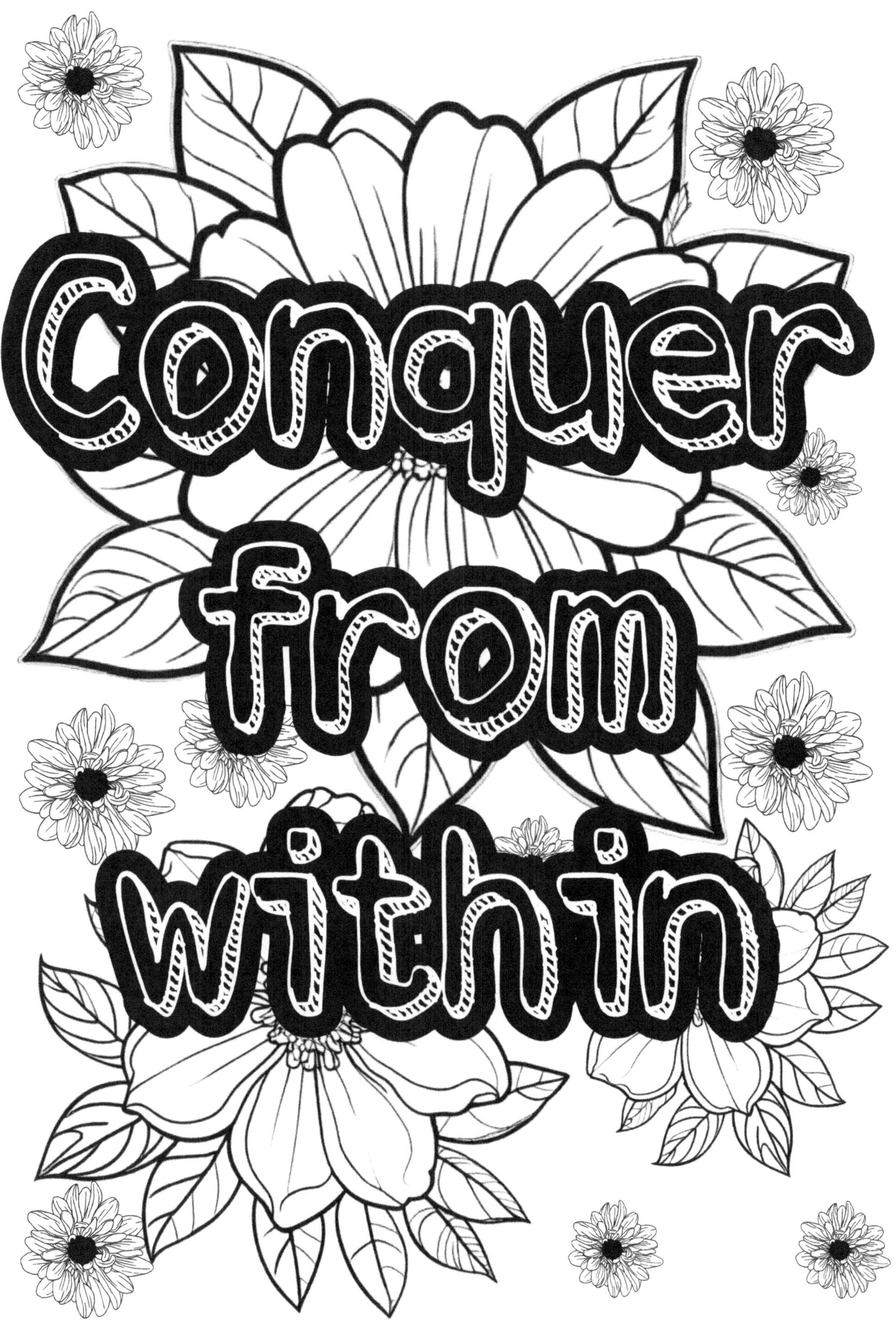

Conquer
from
within

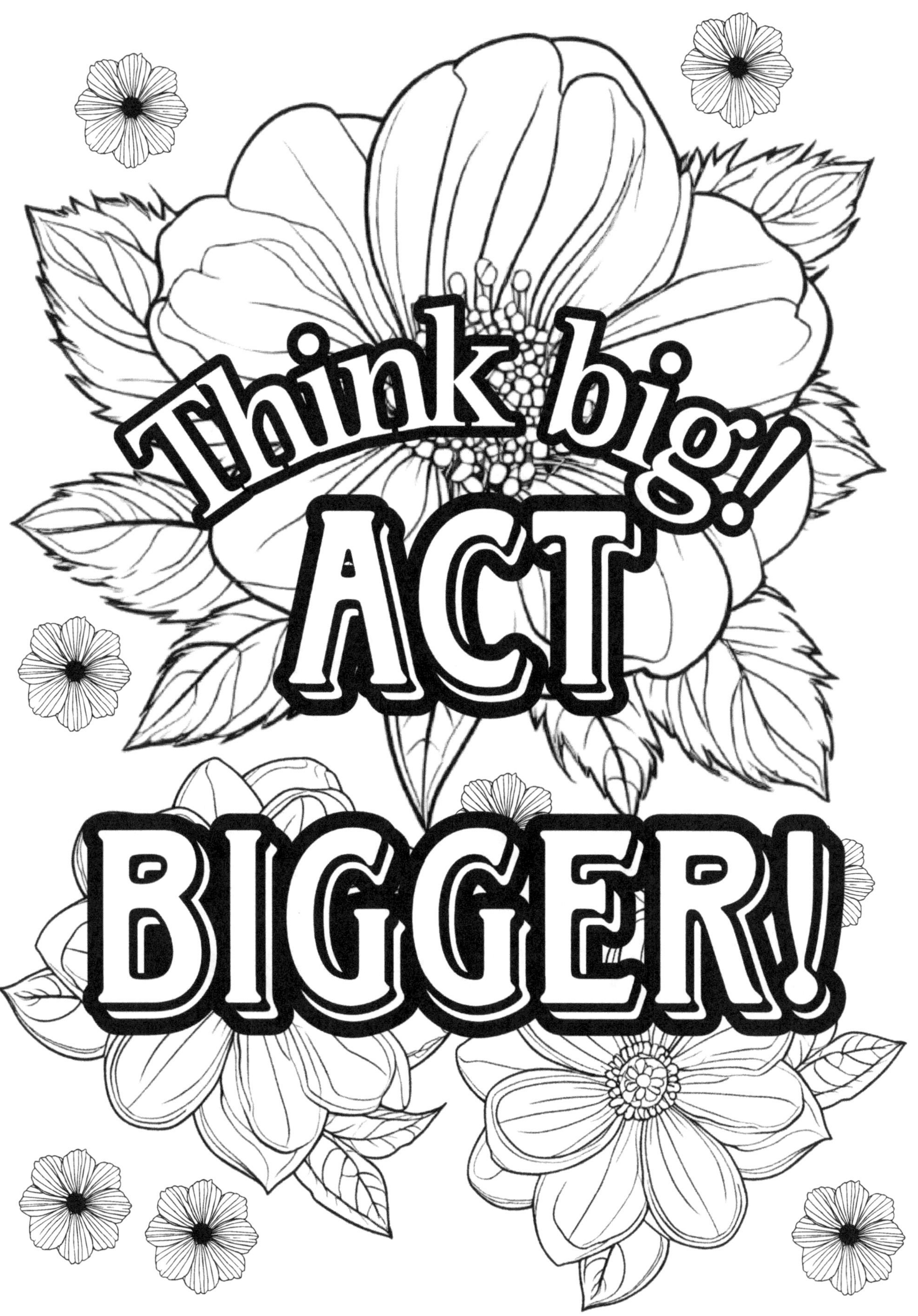

Think big!
ACT
BIGGER!

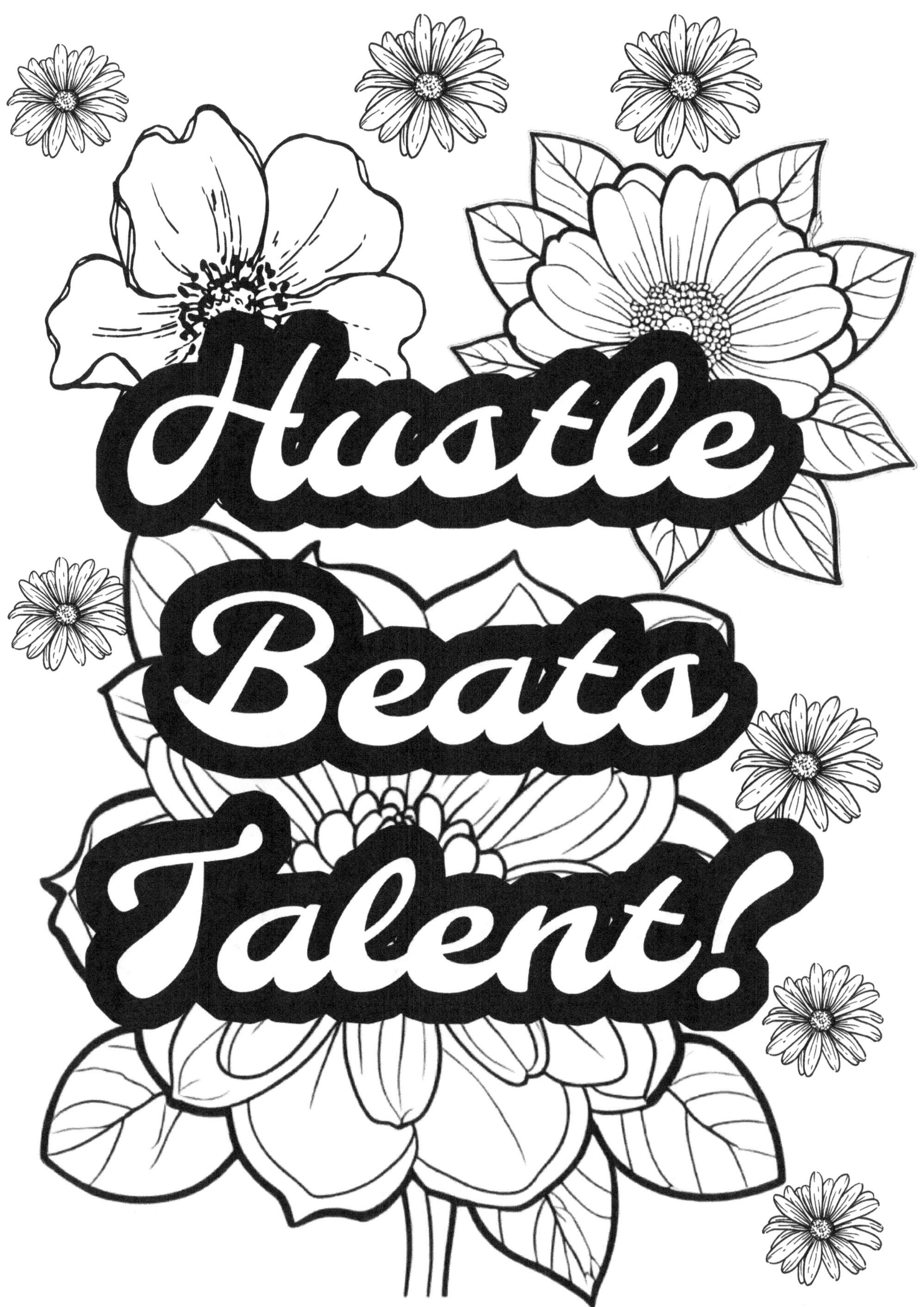

Hustle
Beats
Talent!

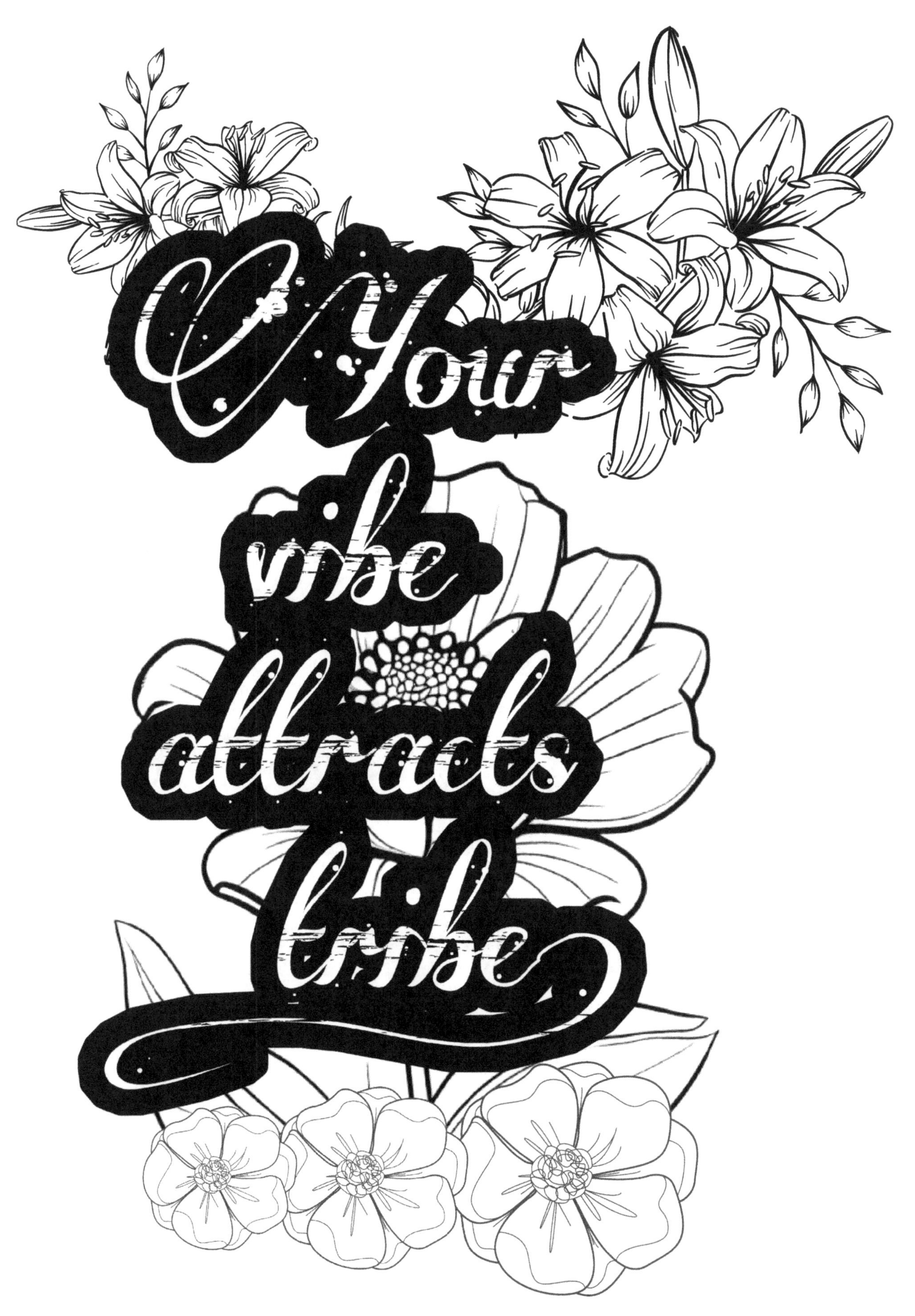

Your
vibe
attracts
tribe

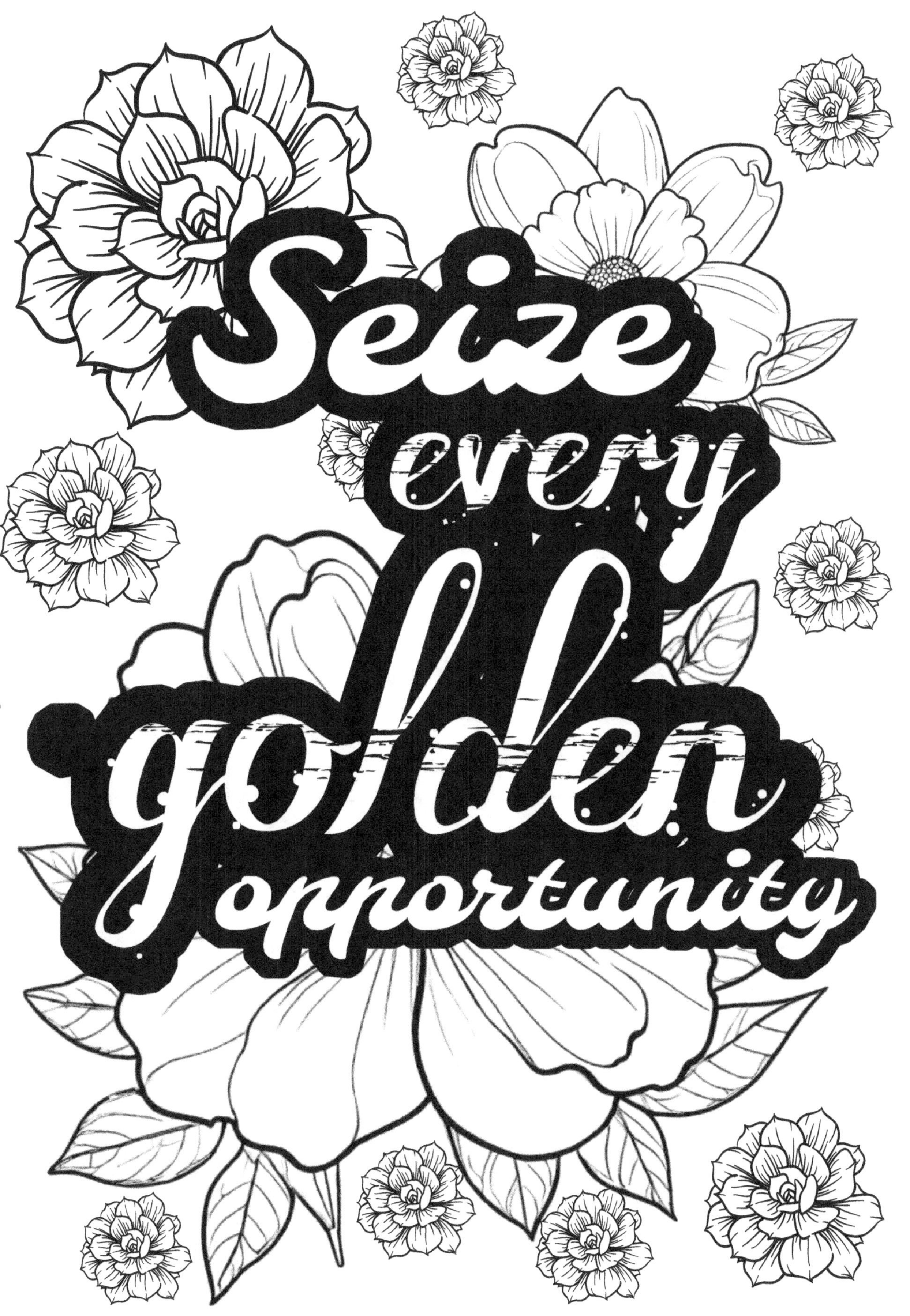

Seize every golden opportunity

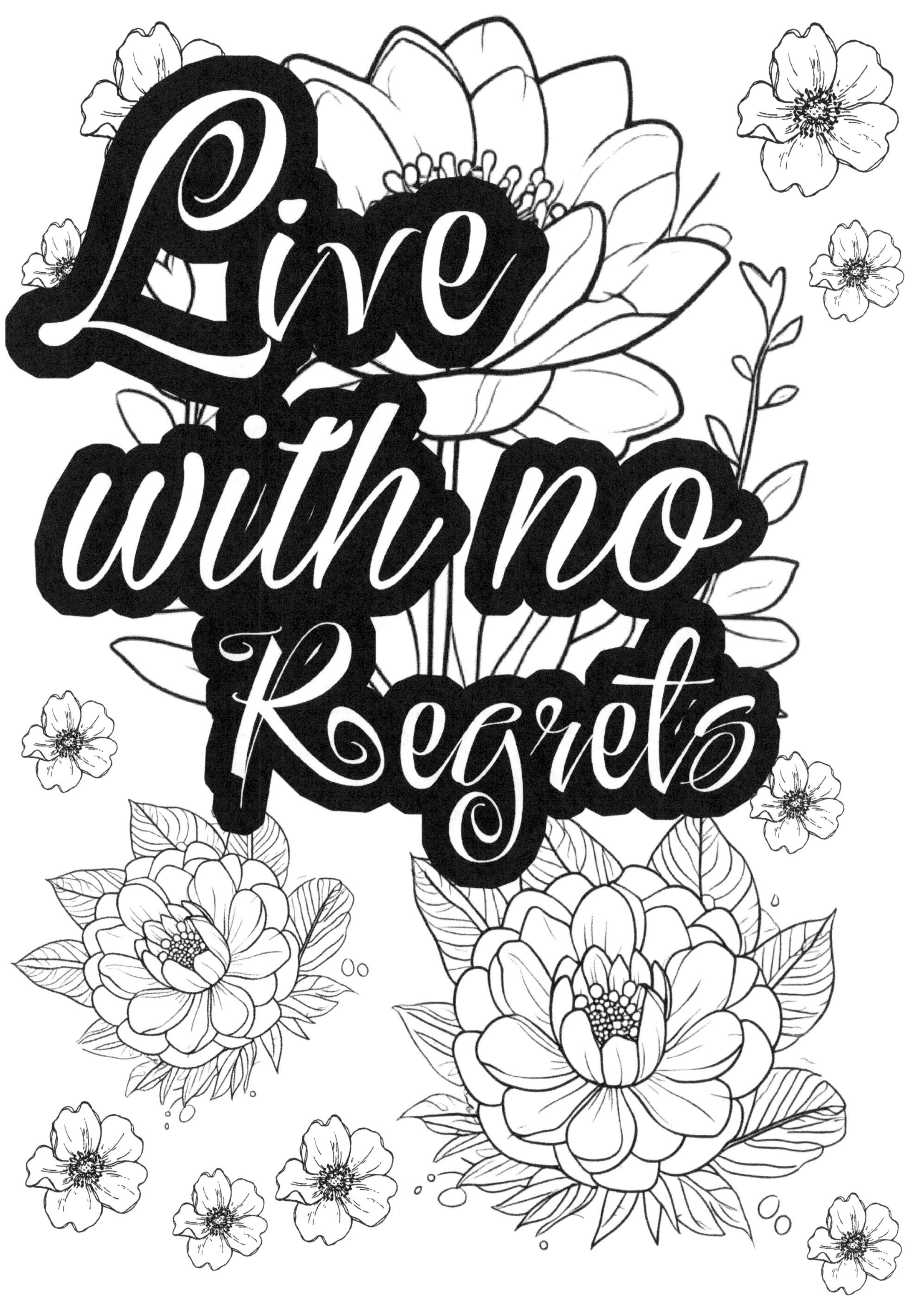

Live
with no
Regrets

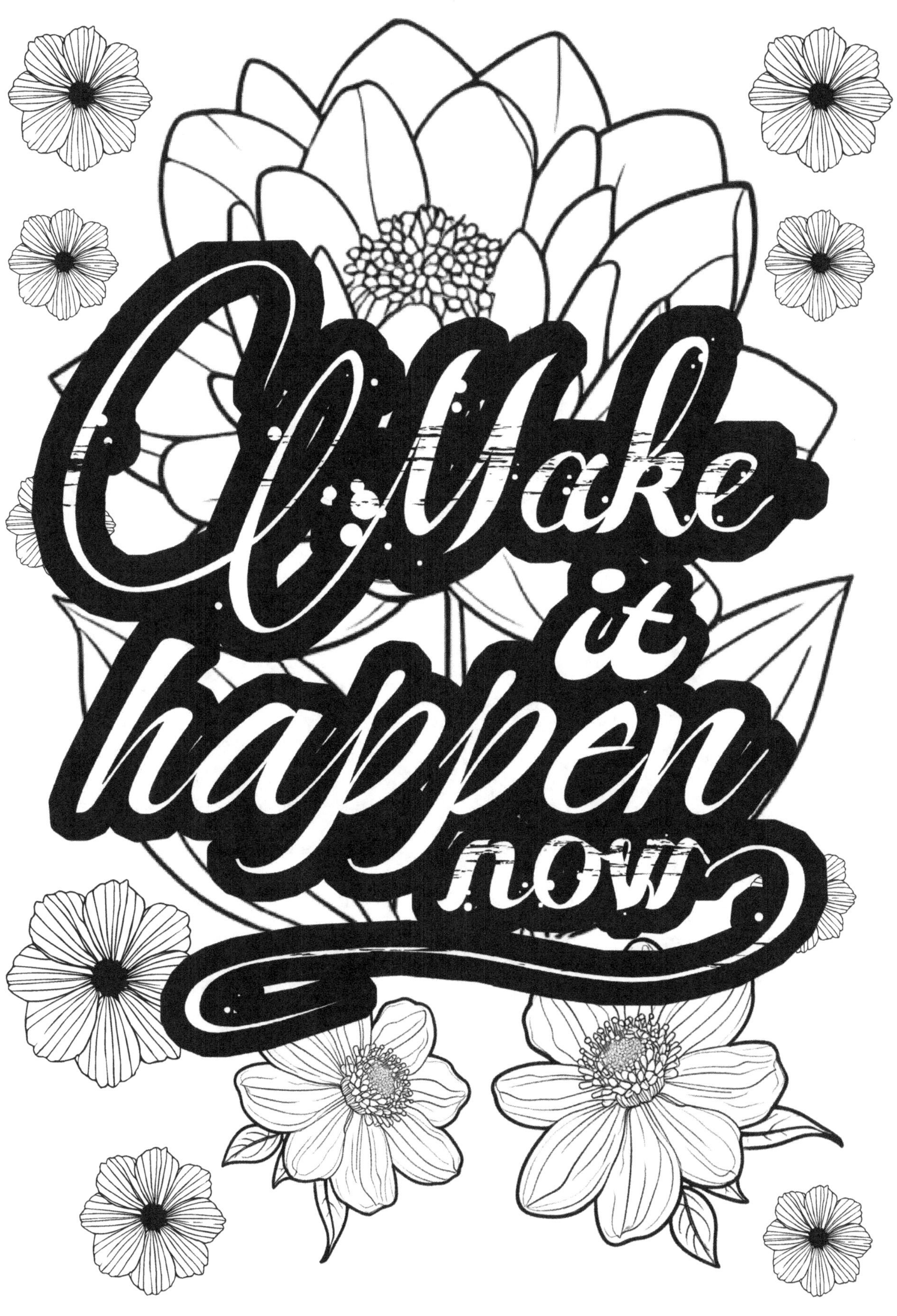

Make it happen now

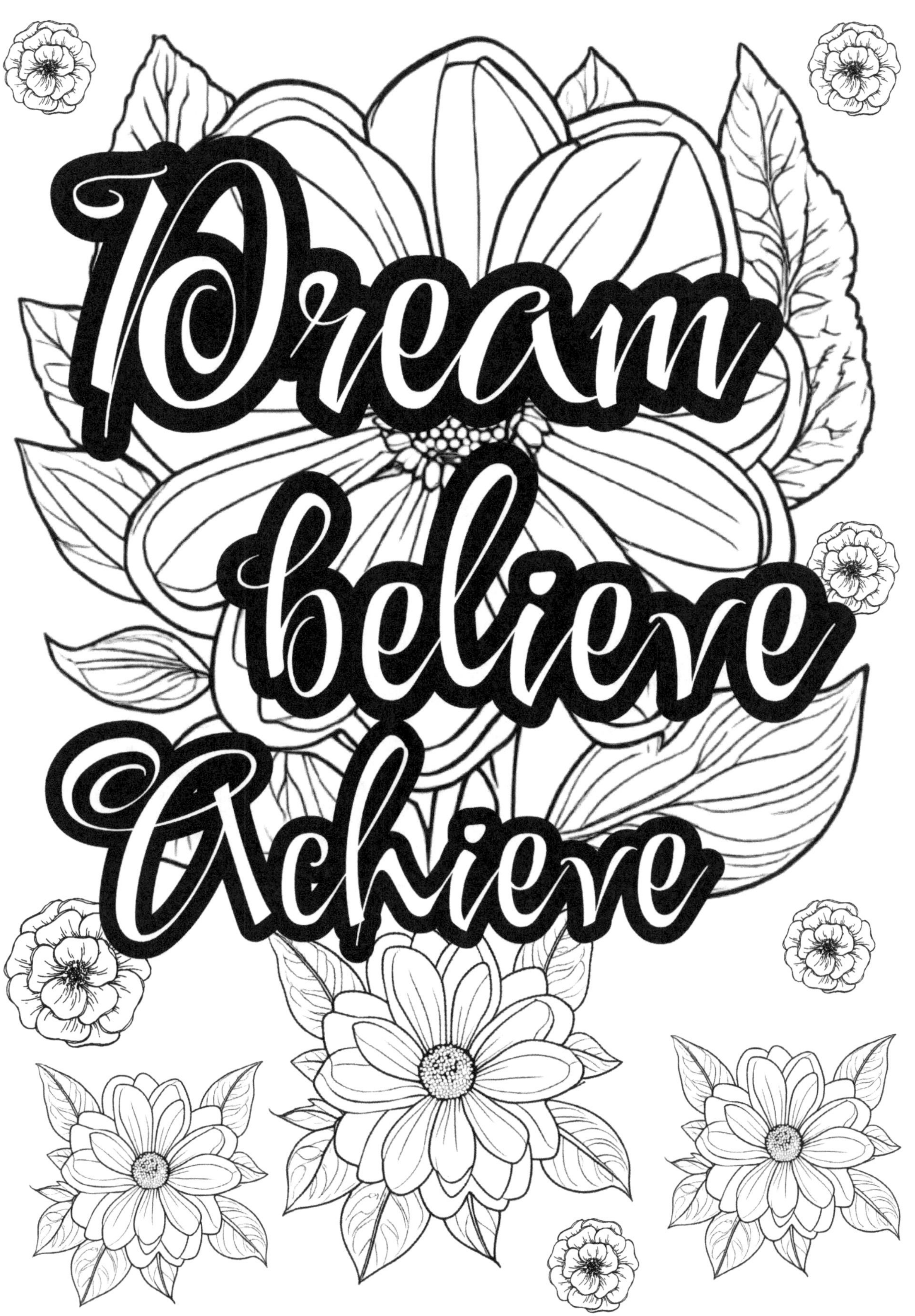
Dream
believe
Achieve

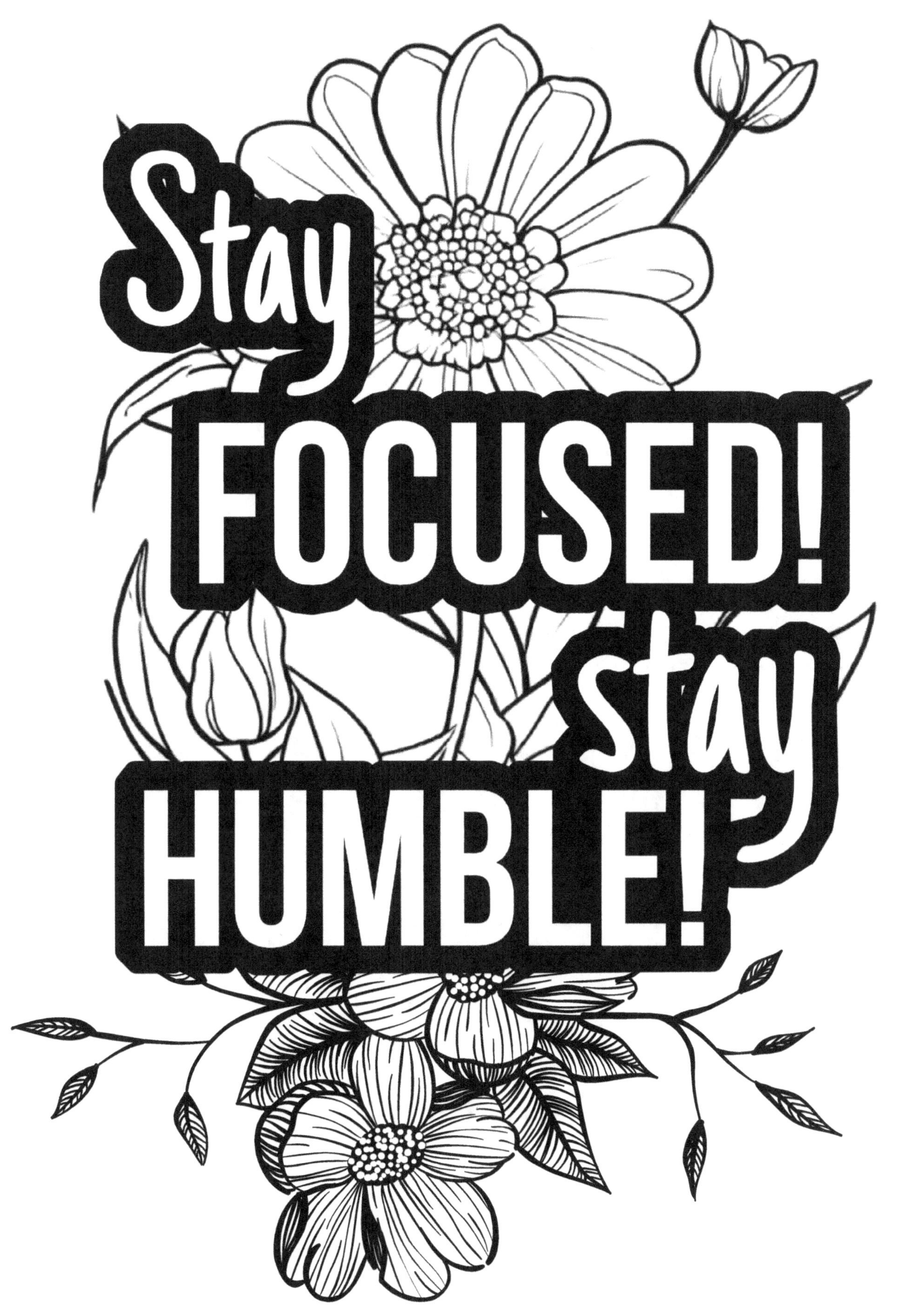

Stay
FOCUSED!
stay
HUMBLE!

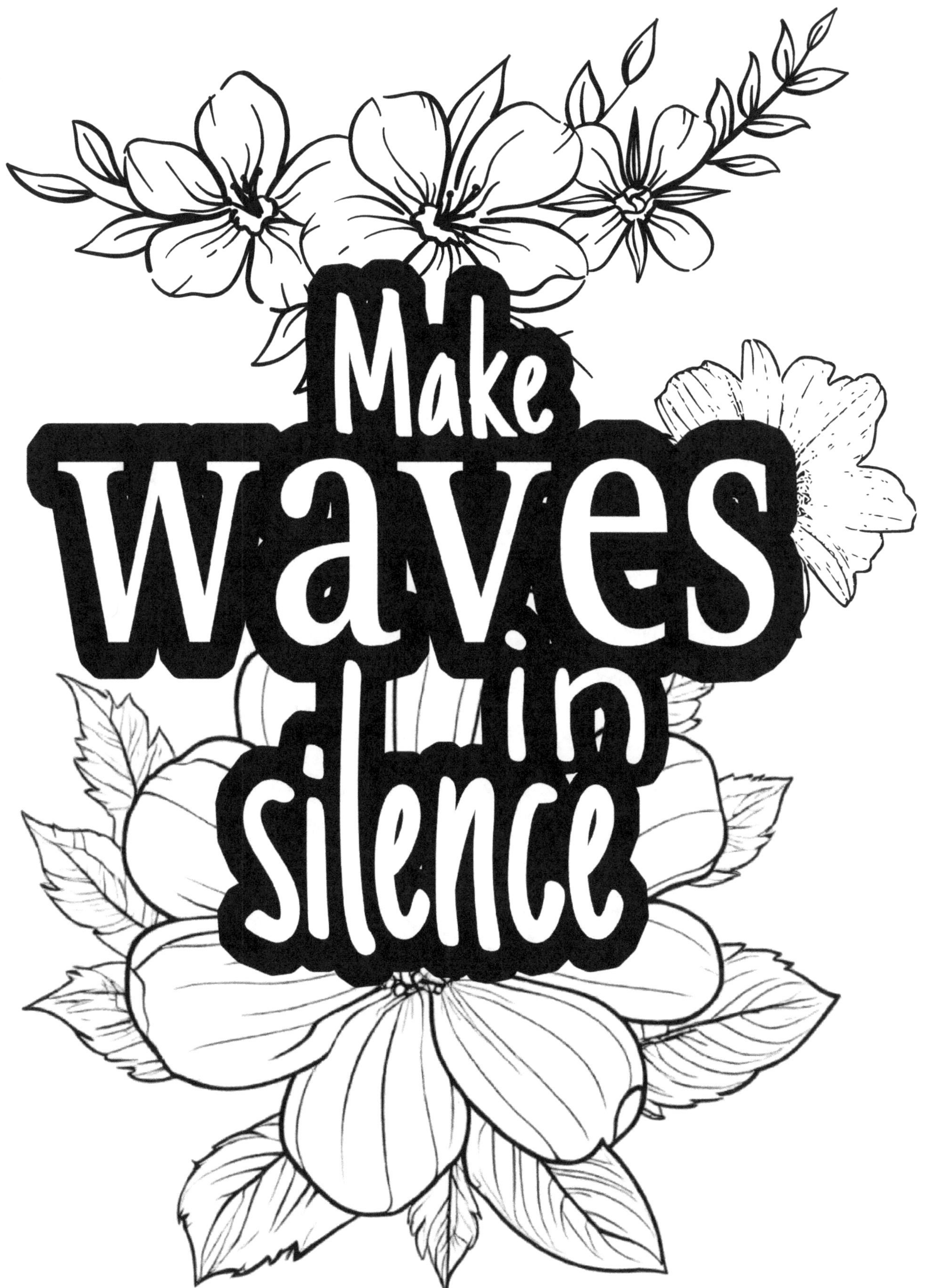
Make
waves
in
silence

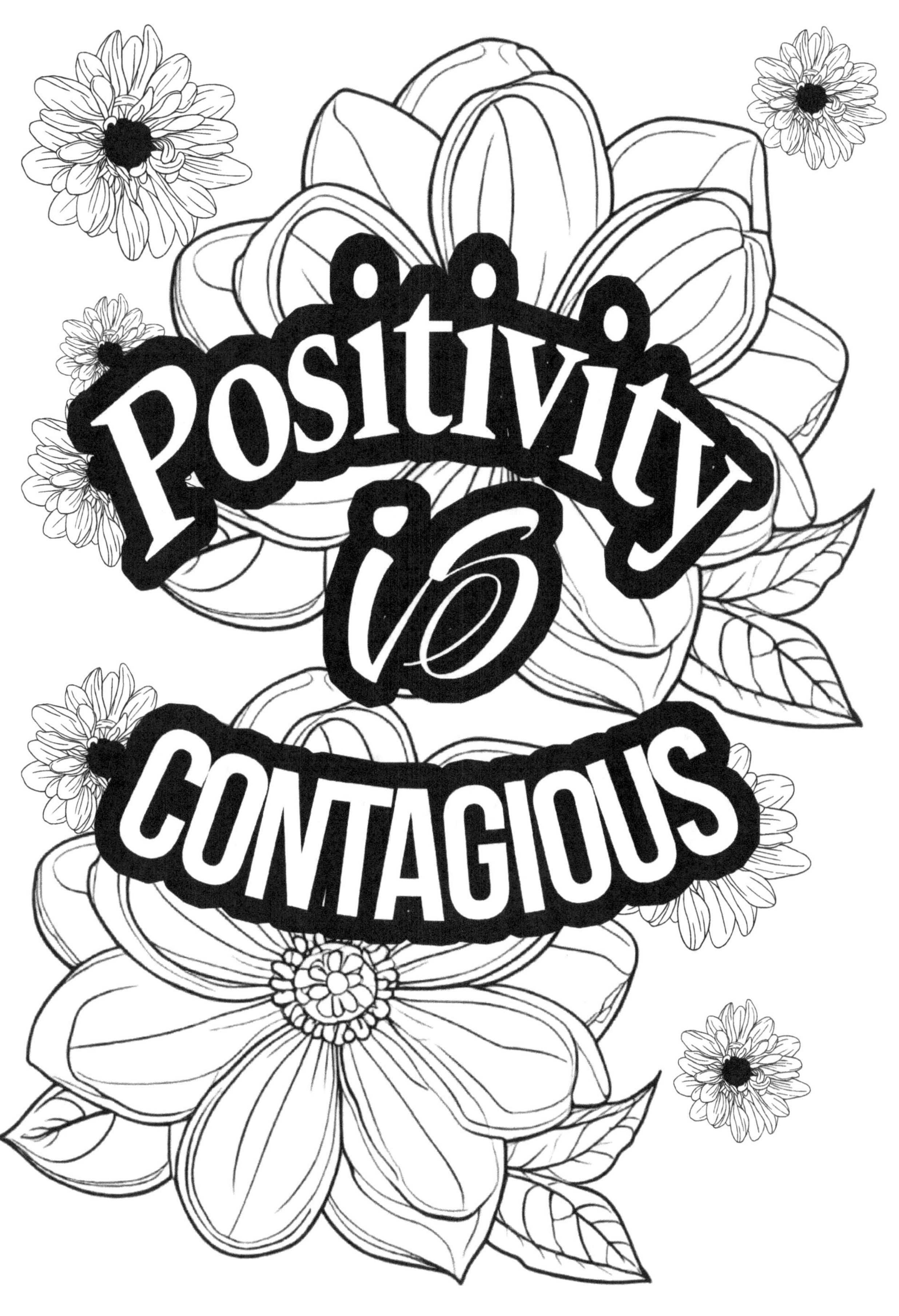
Positivity is CONTAGIOUS

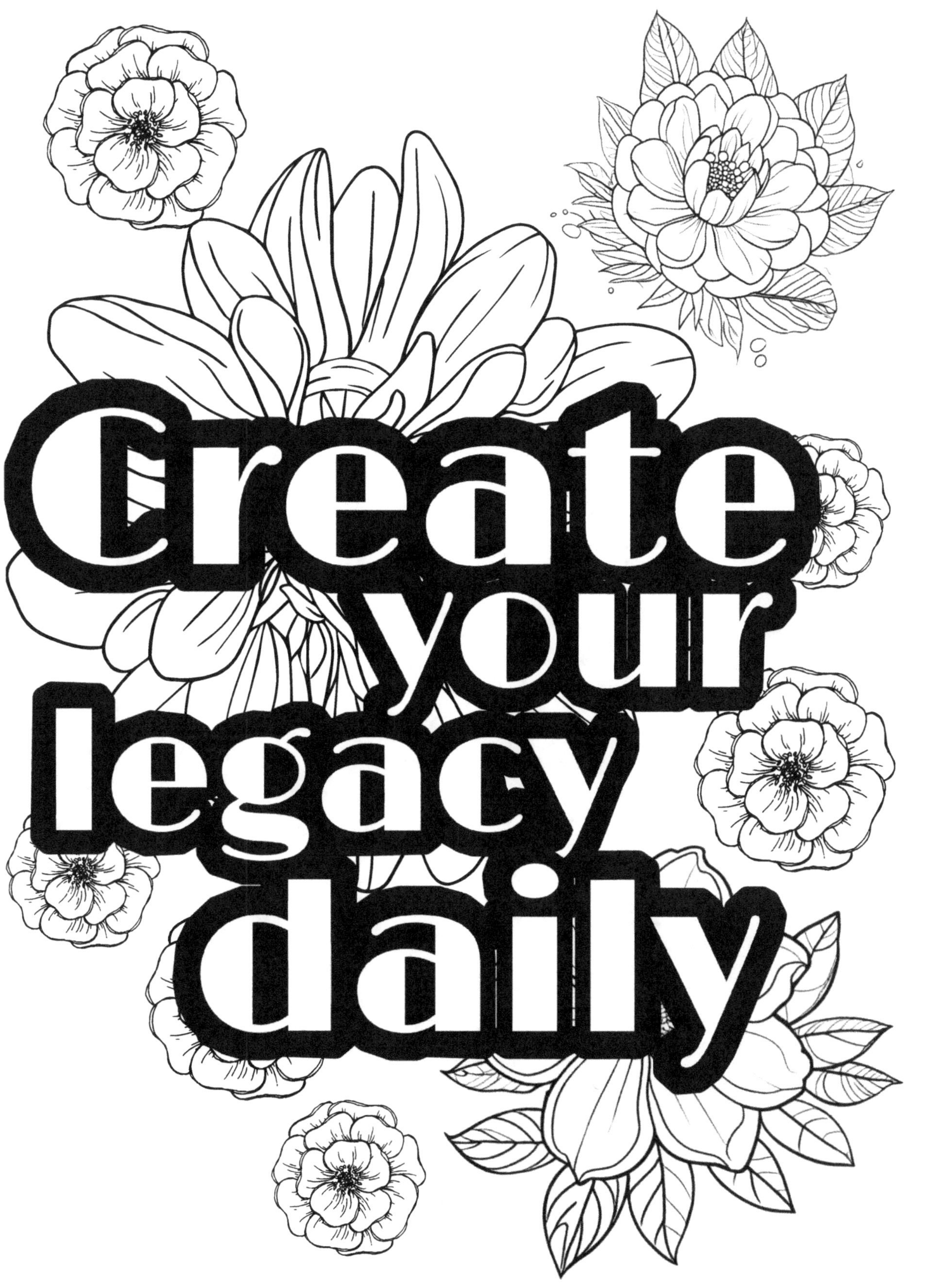

Create your legacy daily

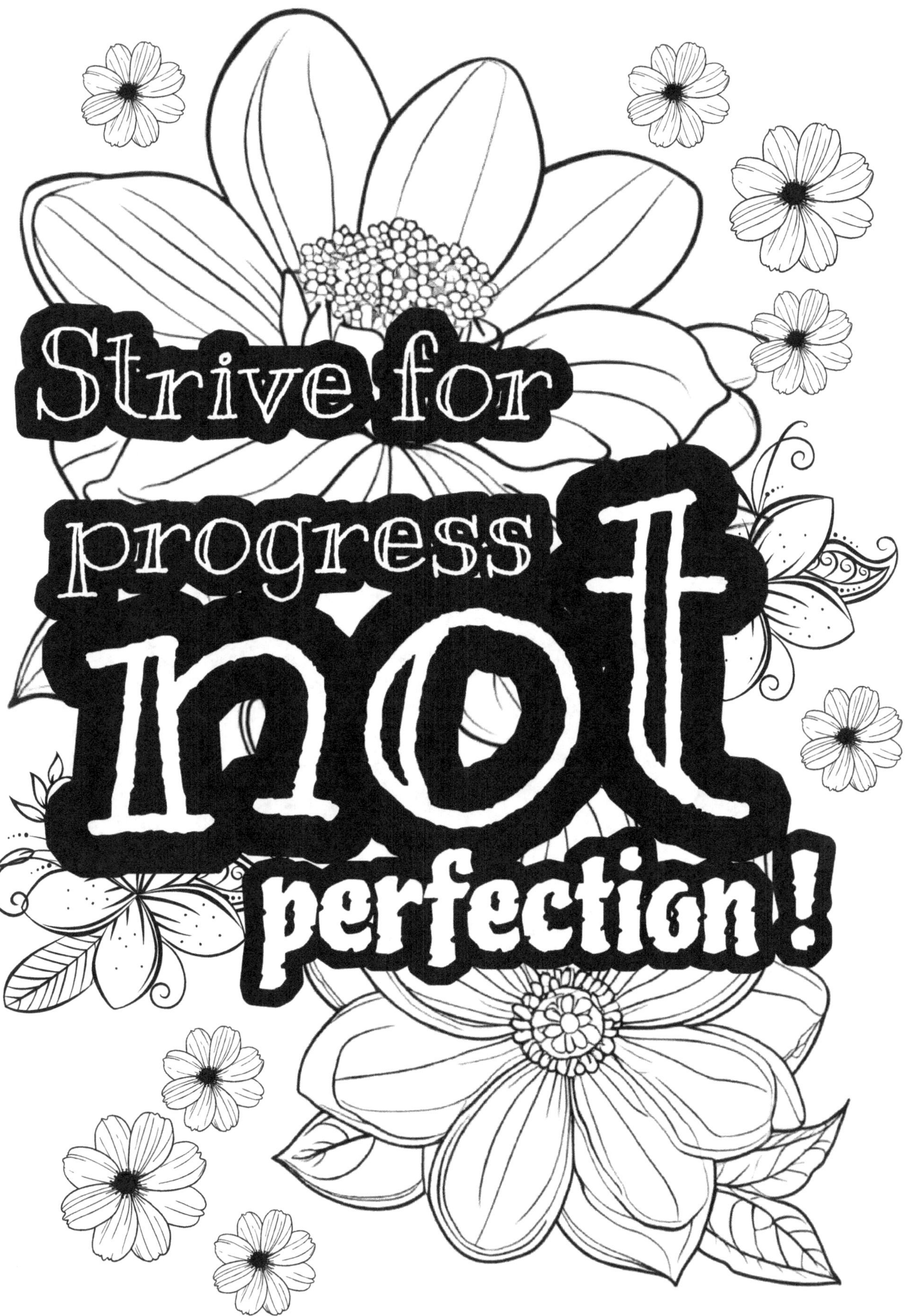
Strive for
progress not
perfection!

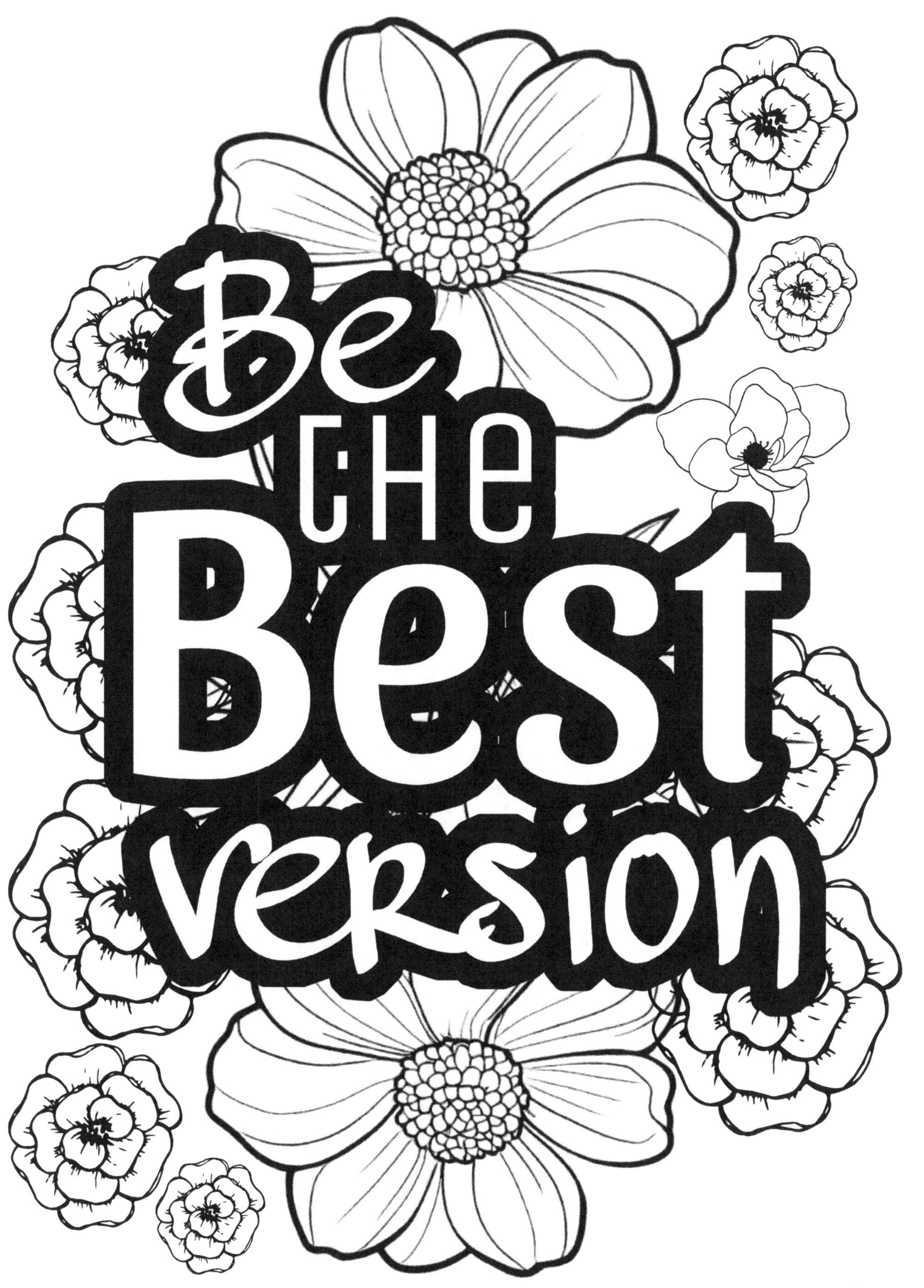
Be
the
Best
version

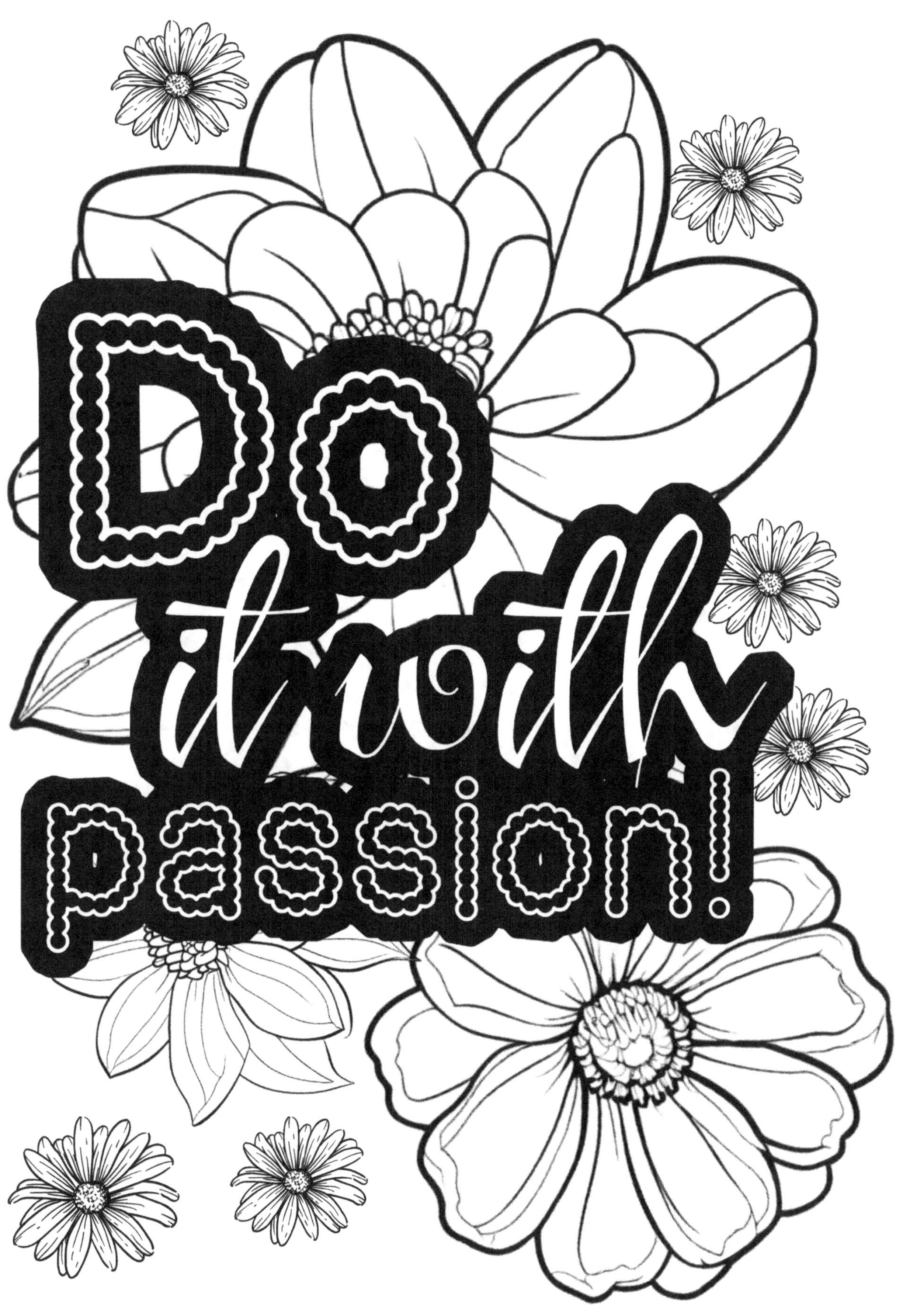
Do
it with
passion!

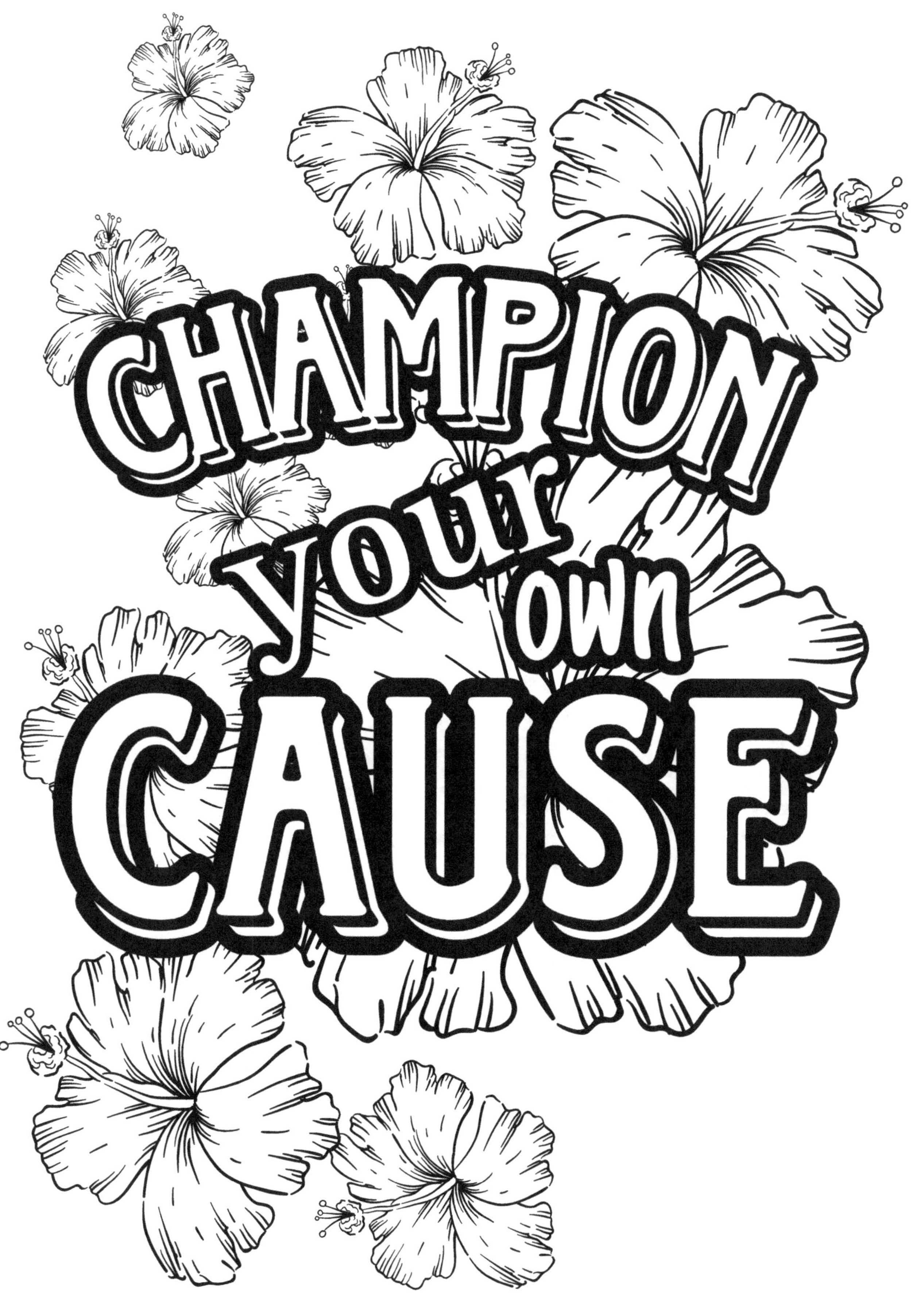

CHAMPION
your
own
CAUSE

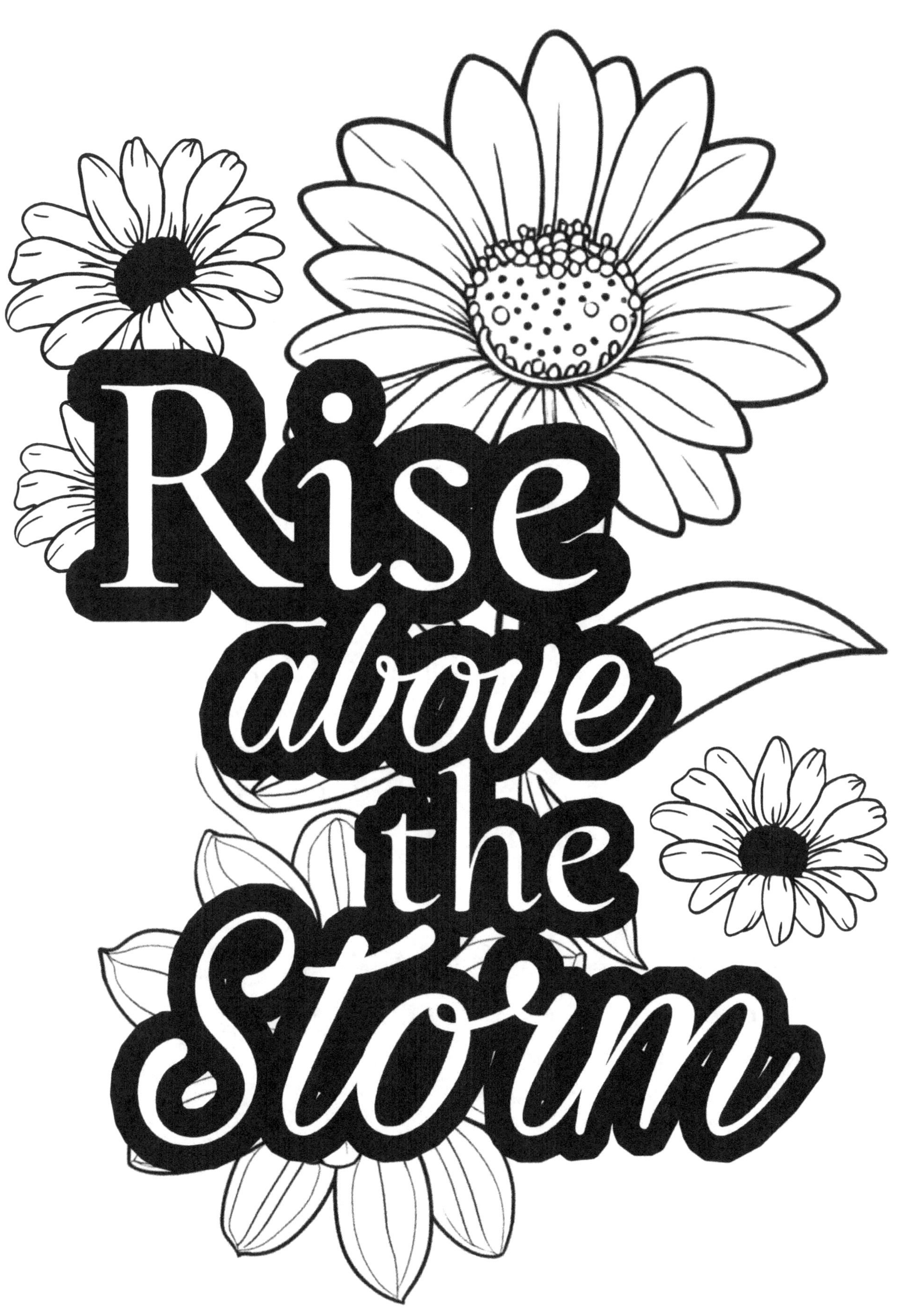

Rise
above
the
Storm

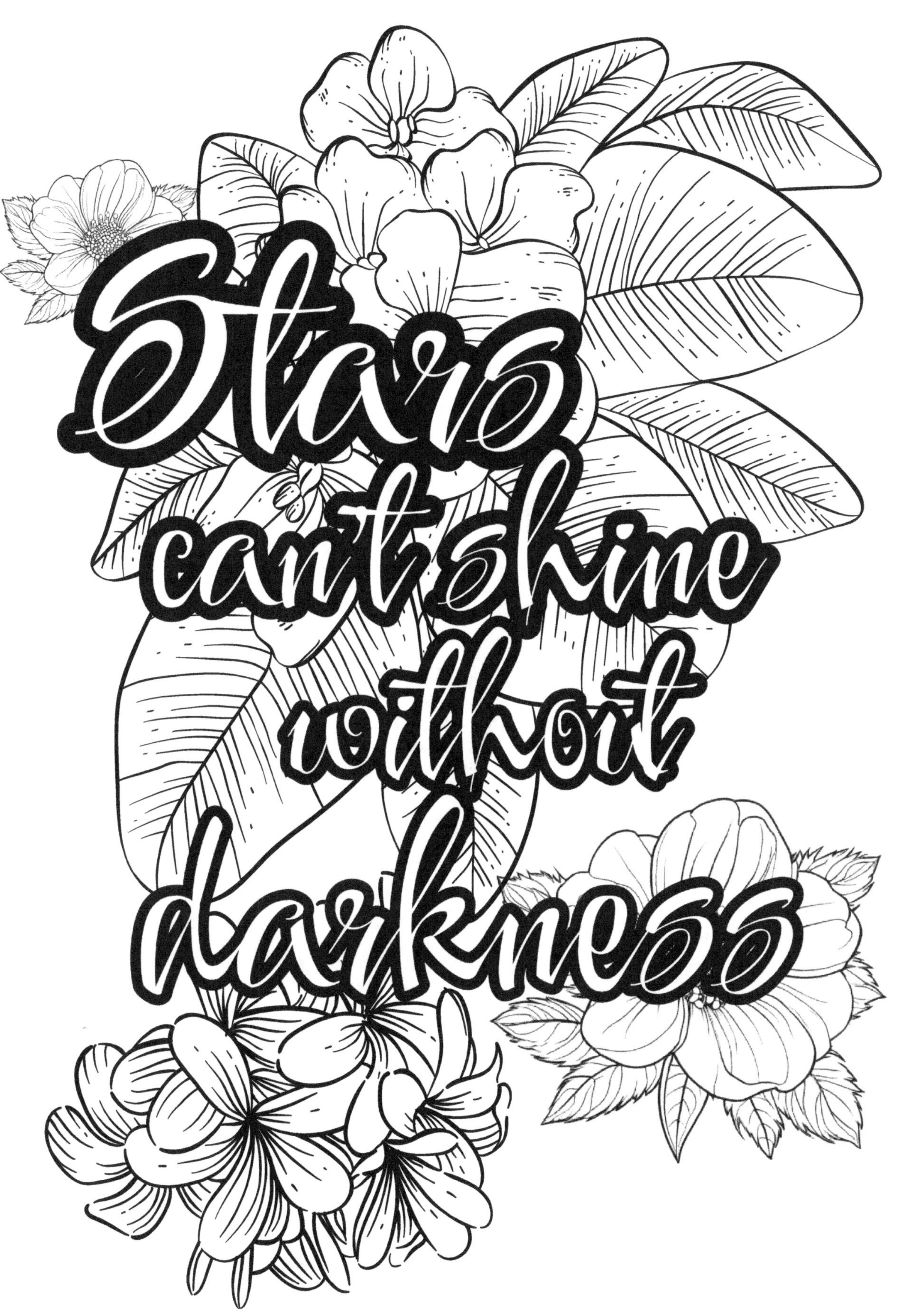
Stars
can't shine
without
darkness

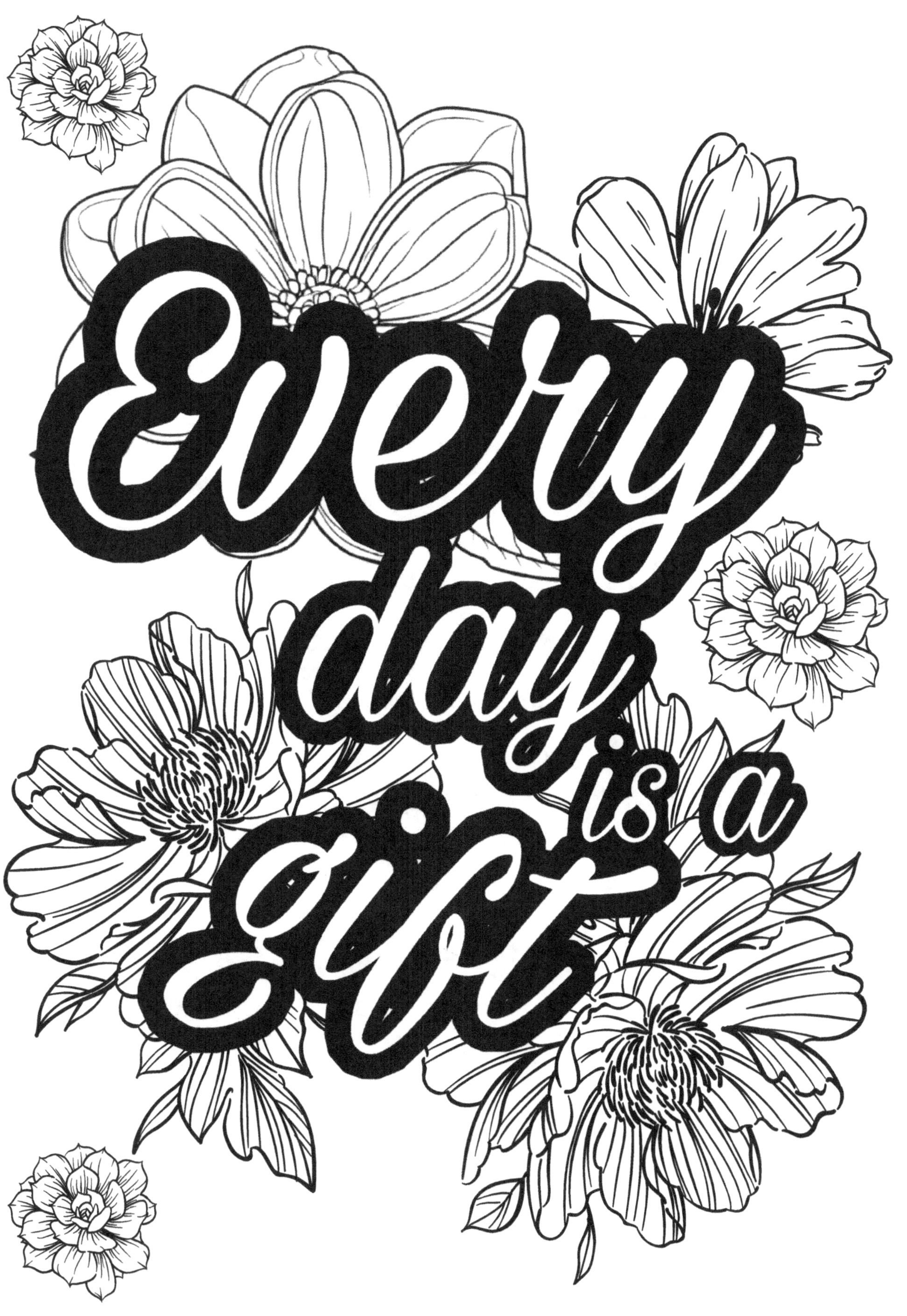
Every
day
is a
gift

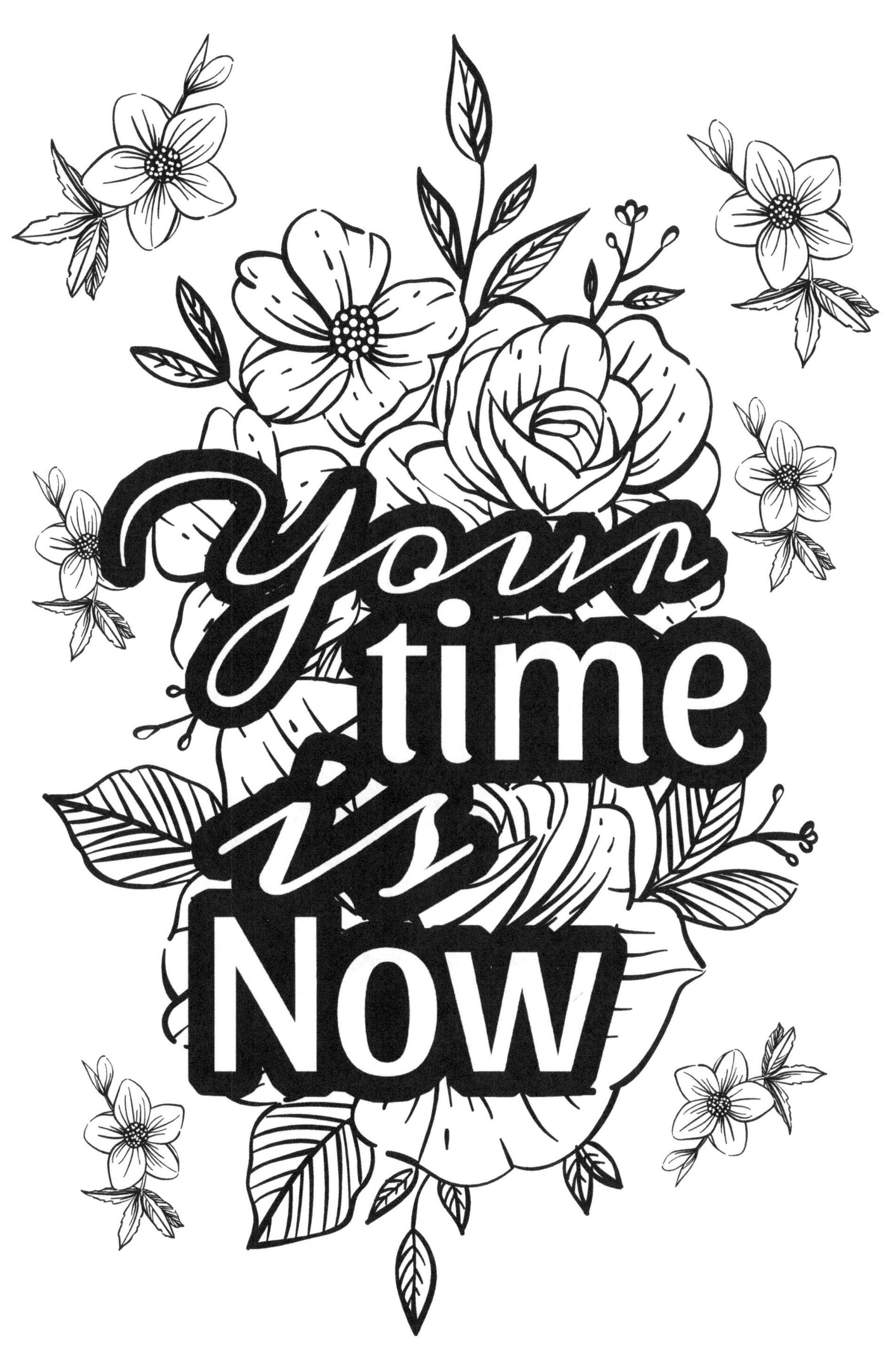

Your time is Now

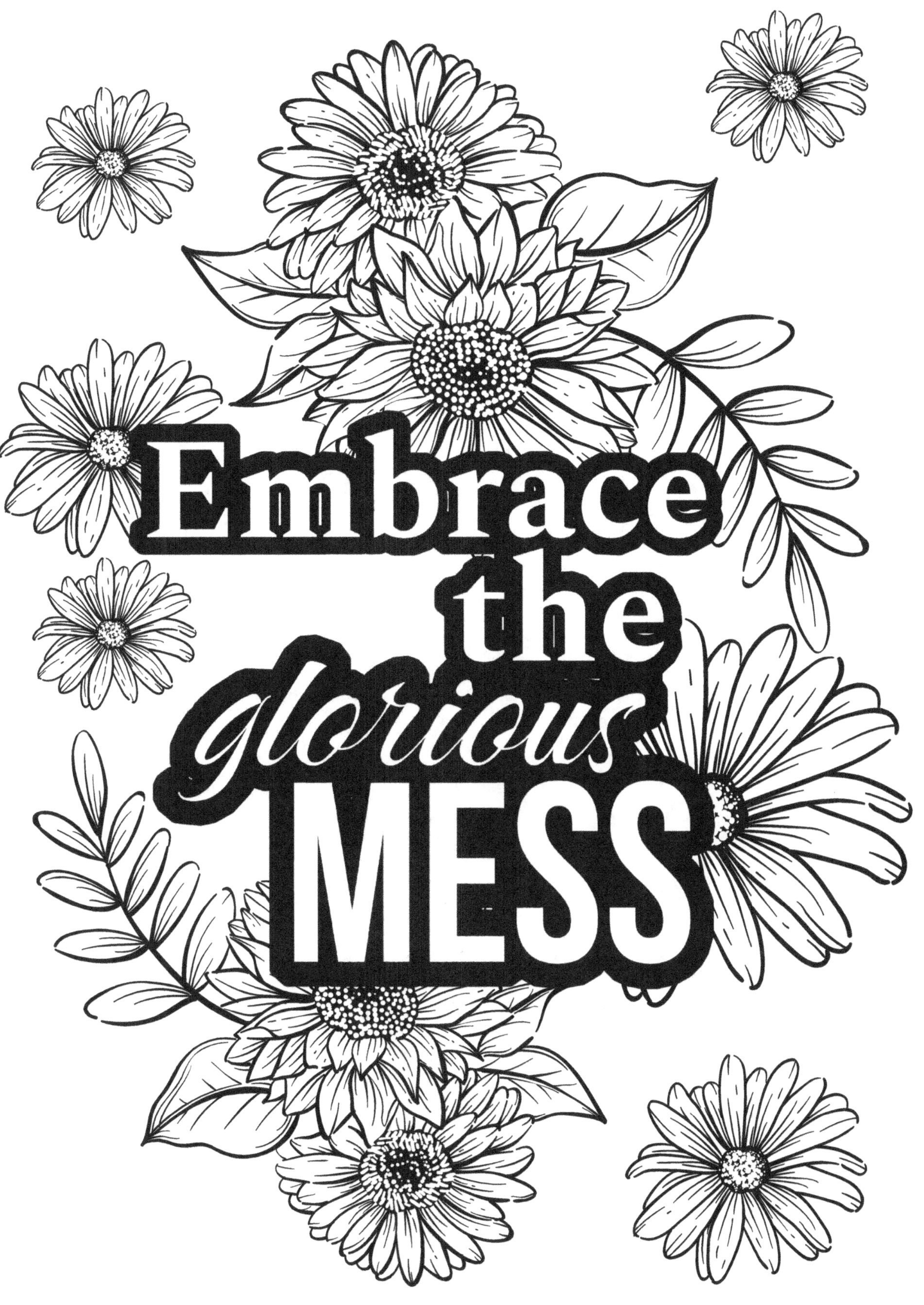

Embrace
the
glorious
MESS